THE
Altar
Guild
MANUAL

Authorized by the Commission on Worship

of The Lutheran Church—
Missouri Synod

Lee A. Maxwell

CONCORDIA PUBLISHING HOUSE · SAINT LOUIS

Copyright © 1996 Concordia Publishing House
3558 S. Jefferson Avenue, St. Louis, MO 63118-3968
Manufactured in the United States of America

Library of Congress Cataloging-in-Publication Data
Maxwell, Lee A., 1955-
    The altar guild manual / Lee A. Maxwell ; authorized by the Commission on worship of the Lutheran Church—Missouri Synod.
        p.   cm.
    Includes bibliographical references and index.
    ISBN 0570048966
    1. Altar guilds—Lutheran Church—Missouri Synod—Handbooks, manuals, etc. 2. Lutheran church—Missouri Synod—Liturgy—Handbooks, manuals, etc. 3. Lutheran Church—Liturgy—Handbooks, manuals, etc.   I. Lutheran Church—Missouri Synod. Commission on Worship.   II. Title.
BX8067.A77M38   1996
247'.08'8241—dc20   96-32525

7   8   9   10   05

Contents

Introduction

The purpose of this book, *The Altar Guild Manual,* is indicated in the last word of its title: *manual.* By definition a manual is a handbook, a book designed to give information about a subject or guide a person through a procedure. That, in essence, is the intent of this book. It is to give information about the altar, the chancel, and the place where the congregation is gathered for services. It is also to be a guide in the procedures for taking care of the objects and places in God's house and for preparing them for the services held there.

For whom is this book written? It is written, first of all, for the altar guild, that group of people in a congregation who have been given the responsibility to do the things mentioned above. The informational and practical intent of the book was developed with them in mind. It is hoped, therefore, that the book will be used by members of the altar guild who are experienced and that it will be useful for helping to train new altar guild members. The book was written, secondly, for those who work most closely with the altar guild, namely, pastors. They should be familiar with the duties and procedures of the altar guild, and this book aims at providing a reference and guide for them as well. Concerning this second intended audience, it is also hoped that this book will be used by seminarians in their liturgical training. If they do not have the opportunity to work directly with an altar guild on their vicarage, they certainly will after they are ordained and installed in their first congregation.

For many years the standard guide and reference for altar guilds and pastors has been Paul H. D. Lang's *What an Altar Guild Should Know.* I am deeply indebted to that work, not only because it was the book used when I had my liturgical training at the seminary, but also because it has provided the basis and points of departure for many of the discussions in this present volume. Lang's work, however, was first published over 30 years ago (1964), with a revised edition several years later (1968). A lot has happened in the areas of church architecture, liturgical practice, and congregational life since that time. I hope that this book addresses newer elements that have become established as well as traditions that have been preserved in the church to this day.

A few words need to be said concerning the directions given in this book. The first word is *adiaphoron.* This word is a Greek term which means "an indifferent thing." It refers to something that is neither commanded nor forbidden in Scripture. Much of what is used in the church or done in its services may be called *adiaphora*. This means that customs and usages will vary from time to time and from place to place. As far as this manual is concerned, not all of the objects and procedures described in it will be used by everyone. Many of them are adiaphora. Yet I felt there was a need to show their place in the church's life and the usefulness they can have for the church today. If nothing else, I did it to underscore the liturgical freedom which Lutheran Christians profess to have.

Nevertheless, there are many customs and usages in the church and its services that have been around for a long time, some since the beginning of the church. These things we call *tradition* in the best sense of the word. Anyone choosing to jettison traditional matters better have a good reason for doing so. Things that the church has selected and retained over her two thousand year history should not be treated lightly and fall victim to the whims or trends of the day. Consequently, it is important to know what is essential and what is not. That knowledge comes only through diligent research and study of the issues.

Perhaps the following may serve as a guiding principle: that which honors God and helps to bring his life-giving Gospel to people. Lang explained this principle well in his book: "Of course, God's Word and Sacraments are not dependent on human embellishment for effectiveness. … [Yet] perhaps we have failed to attract, even alienated, some people by being indifferent to the setting in which we present the Gospel and by tolerating crudities and vulgarities in our churches" (p. 12). This statement, in my opinion, has nothing to do with "high church" or "low church" customs. It has everything to do with the care we take for God's house and the services conducted in it, be the appointments and services simple or ornate. The altar guild has its role in seeing to it that things are done "decently and in order."

With all of this in mind, we can turn to the rubrics or directions given in this book. When the word *should* is used, it is intended to say that the information or guidance given conforms to our confessional Lutheran theology and the best traditions of the church. Of course, *should* is not absolute; circumstances may suggest an alternative. The words *may* and *can* allow more freedom. While the appointment or custom under discussion is in harmony with our theology (or, at the least, does not contradict it), it is a matter left to the judgment of the pastor and/or congregation. This area is where the concept of adiaphora is truly at home! Finally, there is the word *must*. The instances where this word applies are few: The Word of God must be proclaimed; water must be used in Holy Baptism; bread and wine must be used for the Sacrament of the Altar. In view of what was said above, however, this freedom should not be used as license for "anything goes." The wisdom and practice of the orthodox church catholic *should* be taken into consideration.

How should this book be used? Parts I–VI contain background and reference material with which the members of the altar guild should be familiar. This material is perhaps best used by simply having the members of the guild read it. Part VII contains practical instructions for the seasons and services of the church. This material lends itself to review by the guild as a whole in preparation for a particular season and its services. For example, at its January meeting the guild could review the sections on Lent and Holy Week and the services that will be conducted in these seasons, noting particularly the changes that occur during this time. Whatever method an altar guild chooses, it would be beneficial to review all the sections of the book over a period of time.

Two other books deserve to be mentioned which would be beneficial for the altar guild to study and have available in their or the church's library. One of these is *Lutheran Worship: History and Practice*, edited by Fred L. Precht (St. Louis: Concordia Publishing House, 1993). The entire book is worth studying but especially helpful are the following sections: Chapter 2: Corporate Worship of the Church; Chapter 5: The Church Year; Chapter 6: The Setting of the Liturgy and the Decorum of Its Leaders; and Chapter 12: The Divine Service. The other work is *The New Westminster Dictionary of Liturgy and Worship*, edited by John Gordon Davies (Philadelphia: Westminster Press, 1986). Many topics in this volume can quickly be studied or easily be referenced when questions arise.

In addition to the Rev. Lang, there are many others who have contributed to the production of this volume with their patience and wisdom. I thank the Rev. Dr. Fred L. Precht, past executive director of the Commission on Worship; the Rev. Dr. Roger D. Pittelko, the chairman of the Commission on Worship; the Rev. Karl D. Bachman (especially for Appendices B and C), pastor of St. Paul International Lutheran Church of Tokyo, Japan; the Rev. William C. Weedon, pastor of St. Paul Lutheran Church of Hamel, Illinois; and the members of the altar guild of Berea Evangelical Lutheran Church, St. Louis: Irma Bosley, Elsie Fey, Donna Hoffmann, Shirley Lawless, Janice Muckey, Viola Rehg, Lucy Sprenger, and Linda Watts.

May this work bring glory to God and assist in bringing his life-giving Gospel to his people.

Lee A. Maxwell

1

Purpose

God of all grace and mercy, bless those who serve as members of the altar guild that they may be faithful in their service. Grant them steadfast devotion and strong faith. By their loving service to your house of prayer and your altar of worship may your church be built up to the praise and honor of your most holy name; through Jesus Christ, who lives and reigns with you and the Holy Spirit, one God, now and forever. Amen.[1]

This prayer is used in the *Lutheran Worship Agenda* for the placing of altar guild members as servants of the congregation. It expresses three things about the nature of the work of the altar guild: Its purpose is to serve. Its service requires spiritual commitment. And its service has a spiritual goal.

Throughout the history of the Christian church there have always been those who have attended to the place of worship, its furnishings, and its appointments. This service is a needed service. Of course, the pastor himself could do the things the altar guild does, and in some very small parishes he may. But much of the work of the altar guild does not require the knowledge and skill of the pastor. Indeed, there may be others in the congregation who have the abilities required for the service of the altar guild in a greater degree. Moreover, the altar guild's service, as we have come to understand it today, is not something that has been given to the pastor in the Office of the Holy Ministry. In fact, it is an auxiliary service of the type that has been given to others since the earliest days of the church (cf. Acts 6:1–6).

The altar guild is to *serve*. It serves by making sure that the place of worship is maintained and set up for the times and seasons of the church year. It serves by seeing to it that the paraments and linens are put out, cleaned, and stored appropriately. It serves by setting in order, cleaning, and putting away the sacramental vessels and linens. It serves by caring for the vestments of the congregation. It serves by making certain that all the preparations are made for each service and that whatever needs to be done after the service is taken care of. It serves by ordering supplies. It serves by studying topics related to worship and by undertaking projects such as making paraments and vestments. All this, not for themselves, but for the glory of God and the building up of his people.

From the foregoing we can begin to understand how extensive the work of the altar guild may be. There are many things that must be done in preparation for the Divine Service besides turning on the lights and sweeping the floor. The service the altar guild renders is needed and valuable. In most Lutheran churches this service is rendered by some of the women of the congregation. But in centuries past most of the duties done by today's altar guilds were done by men, sometimes even the clergy. Accordingly, there is nothing standing in the way of men serving on altar guilds today. Likewise, there are no barriers of age. Young and old alike may serve the church in this area.

The one special requirement for serving on the altar guild is *spiritual commitment.* The members of the altar guild, first and foremost, are serving God. It is his house. And they are serving God's people. It is they whom God gathers around Word and Sacrament. Their work, therefore, involves the spiritual life of the congregation. They assist the congregation in its worship. Consequently, the members of the altar guild should be devoted to their tasks, be reliable in carrying out their assignments, be humble and reverent in their work, and be joyful for the privilege they have in serving their Lord.

Finally, the work of the altar guild has a *spiritual goal.* It is for the glory of God's name and the building up of his people. To attain this goal three principles must be kept in mind.[2] The first principle is that everything done in a church service is to aid the communication of the Gospel. Nothing is to detract from the centrality of God's Word and Sacraments by focusing on man's pleasure and entertainment. This does not mean that a thing of beauty or splendor cannot be used in the church. On the contrary, God commanded certain things in the Old Testament to beautify the tabernacle and then the temple. So it must be among God's New Testament people where he has deigned to be present. But whatever is done or used in the church must glorify God and serve God's work of strengthening his people in faith and love.

The second principle is that traditional forms and customs of worship are to be kept as long as they are helpful and in harmony with the principle enunciated above. Besides expressing the continuity of the congregation's worship with that of the church throughout history and the world, this principle is what the Confessions of the Lutheran Church testify to: "No conspicuous changes have been made in the public ceremonies of the Mass. … After all, the chief purpose of all ceremonies is to teach the people what they need to know about Christ."[3] If this chief purpose is lost, then the ceremony must be set aside or purified of whatever corruption is associated with it. This principle applies to furnishings, appointments, vestments, and the like.

The third principle is that, while God has commanded his Word to be preached and the Sacraments to be administered, he has not given detailed instructions about the externals of worship. Again, we listen to the Confessors of Augsburg: "Those usages are to be observed which may be observed without sin and which contribute to peace and good order in the church. ... Yet we accompany these observances with instruction so that consciences may not be burdened by the notion that such things are necessary for salvation."[4] Consequently, we cannot be legalistic about certain externals. We cannot say "It has to be done this way" or "It cannot be done that way." Anything that is not commanded or not forbidden by God must be left in the area of Christian freedom.

Customs and forms will differ from time to time and from place to place. Some congregations will have simple customs and furnishings, others will have more elaborate ones. In whatever setting an altar guild is called to work, its members will want to recall the purpose of the work of the altar guild: to serve, to serve with spiritual commitment, and to serve toward a spiritual goal.

Notes

1. *Lutheran Worship Agenda* (St. Louis: Concordia Publishing House, 1984), p. 288.

2. The principles are borrowed and modified from Paul H. D. Lang, *What an Altar Guild Should Know* (St. Louis: Concordia Publishing House, 1964), p. 13.

3. Augsburg Confession, Article XXIV. From *The Book of Concord*, translated and edited by Theodore G. Tappert (Philadelphia: Fortress Press, 1959), p. 56.

4. Augsburg Confession, Article XV; Tappert ed., p. 36.

2

Membership and Organization

It was mentioned in the previous chapter that in most Lutheran churches today only women serve on the altar guild, and that in earlier times in the church the services rendered by what we today call the altar guild were done by men. There is no reason, however, that women and men, of various ages, cannot serve on the altar guild. In fact, participation by men and boys should be encouraged. First of all, the work done by this guild cannot be classified as "women's work." And secondly, the work of the guild in assisting the worship of the congregation in this way is an appropriate avenue of service for any of the "priesthood of the baptized," be they male or female.

Some of the duties of the altar guild may require special knowledge or skills, in which case those members of the congregation who have special talents in these areas may be asked to use their gifts for this purpose. However, anyone who would like to serve their Lord in the general work of the guild should be accepted for this service. Most of the duties can be taught to those who have no experience in altar guild work. Besides the spiritual commitment referred to in chapter 1, all that is required is the willingness to learn.

The organization of the altar guild need not be complicated. If desired by the guild or congregation, a simple constitution may be composed. All that may be needed, however, is a set of rules or guidelines for the guild to follow.[1] Any constitution or set of rules should not be too elaborate. The main purpose of such guidelines is to make clear what the purpose and duties of the altar guild are.

One organizational matter that needs to be addressed is that of the officers of the guild. At a minimum there should be a director or chairperson and a secretary/treasurer. The director of the guild is responsible for presiding at its meetings and for assigning the various tasks that need to be done. The secretary/treasurer is needed to keep the records of the guild and to be in charge of the guild's money. Other offices may be established and assigned duties as the altar guild deems necessary.

Members of the altar guild are necessary and valuable servants of the congregation. As such they should be installed for their work as other officers and board/committee members of the congregation are. A suitable rite can be found in the service books of the church.[2]

Notes

1. See the model of "Rules for the Altar Guild" in Paul H. D. Lang, *What an Altar Guild Should Know* (St. Louis: Concordia Publishing House, 1964), p. 19. Lang, of course, assumes that only women will serve on the altar guild, so modifications may have to be made. A good sample constitution can be found in S. Anita Stauffer, *Altar Guild Handbook* (Philadelphia: Fortress Press, 1985), pp. 109–11.

2. For example, the rite "Placing of Servants of the Congregation" in *Lutheran Worship Agenda* (St. Louis: Concordia Publishing House, 1984), pp. 286–89. Lang also offers a rite in *What an Altar Guild Should Know* on pp. 20–21.

3
Meetings

Meeting for the sake of meeting is a waste of time. As with any organization, the question must be asked "Why?" The purpose of the altar guild meeting may be summarized as follows: (1) to hold devotions which coordinate with the season of the church year and foster the guild member's commitment to his or her work, (2) to discuss the work and business of the altar guild, (3) to study topics which relate to the work of the guild, and (4) to consider various projects which the guild may wish to undertake.

The *devotions* and prayers of the altar guild meeting may follow a simple order.[1] A Scripture reading may be read which is appropriate for the time of the church year. A meditation on this reading may be given by the pastor or one of the guild members.

The *business* of the altar guild follows. A simple agenda may include the following: minutes of the last meeting, officers' reports, committee reports, old business, new business, recommendations to other boards and committees of the congregation. Assignments for altar guild tasks may also be made at this time. A written report of this meeting should be made available to the church council or voters' assembly so that the members of the congregation are aware of the work that the altar guild does.

It is also important for members of the altar guild to *study* various topics which relate to their work. These topics may include but are not limited to the following:

the Divine Service

the Sacrament of Holy Baptism

the rite of confirmation

the wedding service

the funeral service

the Offices of Matins and Vespers

the function of acolytes or altar boys

worship in the early church

Luther and worship

Lutheran worship in the 16th and 17th centuries

the history of the decline of Lutheran liturgical worship

the history of worship among Lutherans in America

Lutheran liturgical renewal

the development and meaning of vestments

the significance of liturgical colors

worship furnishings and appointments

the use of symbols

art in the church

music in worship

the church year

customs in Advent/Christmas/Epiphany

customs in Lent/Easter/Pentecost

customs during the Sundays after Pentecost

customs for the minor festivals.

Finally, *projects* which the altar guild might undertake should be part of the meeting of the guild. The guild may decide to make paraments or vestments. It may make other appointments or decorations for the church. It may help the pastor with educating the congregation about worship practices. Whatever its role, the guild should stand ready to assist the pastor so that the liturgical life of the congregation is enriched. This, after all, is the primary purpose of the altar guild.

Notes

1. See Appendix A, "Devotions and Prayers."

4
Times and Seasons

In the Old Testament God appointed certain days and periods of time for his people to observe. These festivals marked the great acts of salvation that God had done for his people. In the New Testament no days or festivals were commanded. Yet the church, in the freedom of the Gospel, has continued the precedent set in the Old Testament of structuring the year around the great acts of salvation that God has done for us in Christ. This structure is called the *church year* or *liturgical calendar.*

The church year was not appointed or laid out in the New Testament. In fact, the New Testament only makes reference to the observance of the first day of the week, the day on which Christ Jesus rose from the dead (Acts 20:7). Very soon, however, came the annual observance of Good Friday and Easter. Next came Pentecost. By the fourth century Christmas was celebrated, and by the sixth century Advent was added. Later on other events in the life of Christ and in the life of the church were added to the calendar. By the end of the first millennium, the outline of the church year as we have it today was in place.[1]

The basic unit of time within the church is the *day.* As noted above, the first day of the week was observed as the Lord's Day because it was on this day that the Lord Jesus rose from the dead. Each Sunday, therefore, is a celebration of the resurrection. The liturgical day, however, does not begin at midnight or at sunrise. It begins at sunset on the evening before. This follows Old Testament practice which derives from the structure of the day that God established at creation: "And there was evening, and there was morning—the first day" (Genesis 1:5).

Since all of our time is the Lord's, we cannot distinguish between Sunday and the other days of the week as the former being "sacred" and the latter "profane." The Old Testament recognized every day as a day of worship with the daily morning and evening sacrifices at the temple and the daily hours of prayer (see, for example, Daniel 6:10). Daily prayer continued in the New Testament (Acts 2:46) and gradually developed into what are called the canonical hours. Lutherans have recognized the importance of continuing this practice by retaining the orders for two of these hours, Vespers (evening prayer) and Matins (morning prayer), and providing daily psalms and readings for them.[2]

The next unit of liturgical time is the *week*. Each day of the week receives its theme from and is sanctified by the celebration of the resurrection on the previous Sunday. In Christian tradition, however, each day of the week also had a special emphasis. Friday, for example, was a day of fasting in remembrance of Good Friday, the day of our Lord's crucifixion.[3] *Lutheran Worship* continues this tradition by suggesting a weekly rhythm for prayer emphases.[4]

The third unit of liturgical time is the *year*. Over the course of this year the major events in the life of Christ are observed and the primary teachings for the life of his church are reviewed. These two emphases correspond to the division of the church year into two parts: the festival half and the nonfestival half. A different way of looking at the church year is to divide it into three *times*: the Time of Christmas, the Time of Easter, and the Time of the Church. Each of these times, in turn, contains one or more *seasons*.

The Time of Christmas begins with the season of *Advent* (see fig. 4.1). Advent is from a Latin word meaning "coming," and its emphasis is on preparation for the coming of Christ. The first part of Advent focuses on the coming of Christ as King and Judge, while the latter part looks to his coming in the incarnation. The mood of Advent, therefore, is one of hope, anticipation, and preparedness. There are four Sundays in Advent, beginning with the Sunday closest to November 30, the Festival of St. Andrew. In the traditional One-Year Lectionary the Third Sunday in Advent was called *Gaudete*, which means "rejoice." Its theme was the anticipation of the joy coming into the world at the nativity.

Because the secular world begins its celebration of Christmas on the day after Thanksgiving and ends it on December 25, there has been some displacement of Advent. In addition to those in the congregation who want to sing Christmas music instead of Advent hymns, there are those who want to decorate the church far in advance of the actual celebration of the nativity. The pressure to do both of these things should be resisted. Advent is too important theologically to shorten or displace it.

The season of *Christmas* begins on the evening of December 24, the Eve of the Nativity of Our Lord, and continues through January 5. The feast day is December 25. On the octave[5] of Christmas two festivals occur: the Circumcision of Our Lord and the Name of Jesus. Depending on the day of the week on which Christmas falls, there may be two Sundays after Christmas. In most years, however, there is only one. Because of the nature of this singular event in the history of the world and its meaning for our salvation, the festival and season of Christmas is a time of great joy.

The third part of the Time of Christmas is the season of *Epiphany*. The Epiphany of Our Lord falls on January 6 and commemorates the visit of the Wise Men to the infant Jesus. Like Christmas, this season begins on the eve of the feast, that is, the evening of January 5. On the Sunday after the Epiphany the church observes the Baptism of Our Lord.

Figure 4.1 Sundays and Major Festivals

The Time of Christmas

Advent Season

> First Sunday in Advent
>
> Second Sunday in Advent
>
> Third Sunday in Advent
>
> Fourth Sunday in Advent

Christmas Season

> THE NATIVITY OF OUR LORD
>
> > *Christmas Eve*
> >
> > *Christmas Dawn*
> >
> > *Christmas Day*
>
> First Sunday after Christmas
>
> Second Sunday after Christmas

Epiphany Season

> THE EPIPHANY OF OUR LORD
>
> The Baptism of Our Lord
>
> > *First Sunday after the Epiphany*
>
> Second Sunday after the Epiphany
>
> Third Sunday after the Epiphany
>
> Fourth Sunday after the Epiphany
>
> Fifth Sunday after the Epiphany
>
> Sixth Sunday after the Epiphany
>
> Seventh Sunday after the Epiphany
>
> Eighth Sunday after the Epiphany
>
> The Transfiguration of Our Lord
>
> > *Last Sunday after the Epiphany*

The Time of Easter

Lenten Season

> Ash Wednesday
>
> First Sunday in Lent
>
> Second Sunday in Lent
>
> Third Sunday in Lent
>
> Fourth Sunday in Lent
>
> Fifth Sunday in Lent

Holy Week

> PALM SUNDAY
>
> > *Sunday of the Passion*
>
> Monday in Holy Week
>
> Tuesday in Holy Week
>
> Wednesday in Holy Week
>
> Maundy Thursday
>
> GOOD FRIDAY

Easter Season

> THE RESURRECTION OF OUR LORD
>
> > *Easter Eve*
> >
> > *Easter Day*
> >
> > *Easter Evening*
>
> Second Sunday of Easter
>
> Third Sunday of Easter
>
> Fourth Sunday of Easter
>
> Fifth Sunday of Easter
>
> Sixth Sunday of Easter
>
> THE ASCENSION OF OUR LORD
>
> Seventh Sunday of Easter
>
> PENTECOST
>
> > *Pentecost Eve*
> >
> > *The Day of Pentecost*
> >
> > *Pentecost Evening*

The Time of the Church

The Season after Pentecost

> The Holy Trinity
>
> > *First Sunday after Pentecost*
>
> Second through Twenty-seventh Sunday after Pentecost
>
> Sunday of the Fulfillment
>
> > *Last Sunday after Pentecost*

Depending on the date of Ash Wednesday, there may be as many as eight Sundays after the Epiphany. The last Sunday after the Epiphany is the Transfiguration of Our Lord. The emphasis of the Epiphany season is on the self-revelation of God to the world. Beginning with the Epiphany, when Christ revealed himself to the Gentile Wise Men as a "Light to lighten the Gentiles," this revelation emphasis continues, as the Gospel readings depict how Jesus revealed himself in word and deed.

The second division of the church year is the *Time of Easter*. The first subdivision of this time is the season of *Lent*. Lent begins with Ash Wednesday, whose precise date depends on the date of Easter (see below). The name "Ash Wednesday" comes from a practice originating in the Middle Ages of ashes being sprinkled over the heads of those who came to church and went to confession. Today ashes are applied to the forehead in the shape of a cross. Ordinarily, the ashes come from palms that were blessed on Palm Sunday the year before. Both this rite and the traditional readings for the day call for an attitude of humility and repentance.

Technically Lent consists of 40 days of fasting. This excludes the Sundays in between which are not Sundays *of* Lent but Sundays *in* Lent. There are five Sundays in Lent. The Fourth Sunday in Lent, according to the traditional One-Year Lectionary, is called *Laetare*, which means "rejoice." This Sunday was apparently introduced to relieve some of the rigors of observing the Lenten fast, but like *Gaudete* in Advent it can be considered anticipatory of the joy of Easter. The season of Lent continues until the eve of Palm Sunday. In the Middle Ages the penitential aspect of Lent was emphasized and the observance of the season was often rigorous and austere. With the revised lectionary included in *Lutheran Worship* the repentance theme is balanced more with reflection and renewal in faith and life.

The second part of the Time of Easter is *Holy Week*. Holy Week begins with Palm Sunday (also called the Sunday of the Passion), which recalls Jesus' triumphal entry into Jerusalem. The three following days, Monday of Holy Week, Tuesday of Holy Week, and Wednesday of Holy Week, look at the events which led up to the crucifixion. Maundy Thursday (also called Holy Thursday) commemorates the institution of the Lord's Supper as a "memorial" of Christ's Passion. On Good Friday (also called Holy Friday) we recall the climactic event in the life of our Lord on earth, the crucifixion. During Holy Week the focus is on the suffering and death of our Savior and the importance that it has for us and for our salvation.

The third and final part of the Time of Easter is the season of *Easter*. Easter is the high point of the church year and has been called the "queen of feasts." The early church recognized the importance of this feast, since it was the first festival to be observed annually by Christians. Easter is the time of greatest joy, because, by the resurrection of our Lord, Jesus proved that he is the victor over sin, death, and the grave.

The date of Easter changes from year to year. This fluctuation is because the date of Easter was originally set according to a lunar (moon) calendar. The moon is still used to set the date of Easter. The formula is as follows: Easter is the Sunday after the first full moon following the spring equinox. The spring equinox falls on March 21. This means that the earliest date Easter can be is March 22, while the latest is April 25.

Easter begins with the celebration of the resurrection of our Lord. Like Christmas and Epiphany, the festival commences already on the Eve of Easter. Easter is followed by six Sundays. The first Sunday following is designated the Second Sunday of Easter and the last is called the Seventh Sunday of Easter. Between the Sixth and Seventh Sundays of Easter is Ascension Day. Ascension Day falls on the 40th day after Easter and commemorates when the risen Lord ascended into heaven. It is always on a Thursday. The conclusion of the Easter season is the Feast of Pentecost, the 50th day after Easter. On Pentecost we commemorate the sending of the Holy Spirit, the Lord and Giver of life, to the disciples who were waiting in Jerusalem after the ascension of Jesus. Because it is through the work of the Spirit that we receive the benefits of Christ's work for us, Pentecost is also a time of great celebration and joy.

The third division of the church year, which actually covers about half of the calendar year, is the *Time of the Church.* The Time of the Church begins with the Sunday of the Holy Trinity, also known as the First Sunday after Pentecost. The following Sundays, until the end of the church year, are then enumerated as Sundays after Pentecost. They were formerly designated Sundays after Trinity, but the usage "after Pentecost" was earlier. To call them Sundays after Pentecost, therefore, is simply a return to an earlier custom. If Pentecost falls early enough, there may be as many as 28 Sundays after Pentecost. The last Sunday after Pentecost is called the Sunday of the Fulfillment or Christ the King.

During the Time of the Church the focus is not so much on the major events in the life of our Lord but on his teaching and how it is applied in the life of the church. Each Sunday, however, remains a celebration of the resurrection, as it is in the Time of Christmas and the Time of Easter. Nevertheless, the intensity of joy and the festivity of the occasion are not as great during the Time of the Church as on the great feasts of Easter and Christmas. This is why in other traditions the Time of the Church is referred to as "ordinary time."

With the end of the church year the cycle begins again. The Time of Christmas. The Time of Easter. The Time of the Church. In another sense, however, all the time of the church year "is now the time after Pentecost."[6] Our Lord has ascended into heaven and has sent his Spirit. We now await the end of time, when our Lord will gather the faithful to celebrate "the marriage feast of the Lamb in his kingdom" which has no time.

Notes

1. For a more detailed explanation of how the church year developed, see Paul H. D. Lang, *What an Altar Guild Should Know* (St. Louis: Concordia Publishing House, 1964), p. 102; or *The New Westminster Dictionary of Liturgy and Worship*, ed. by J. G. Davies (Philadelphia: Westminster Press, 1986), s.v. "Calendar," by R. F. Buxton; see also related articles in the Dictionary, such as "Advent," "Christmas," "Lent," and "Easter."

2. See *Lutheran Worship Altar Book* (St. Louis: Concordia Publishing House, 1982), pp. 127 and 133–36.

3. Lang, p. 103.

4. See *Lutheran Worship* (St. Louis: Concordia Publishing House, 1982), p. 294.

5. An *octave* is an eight-day period beginning with the festival day. The eighth day, exactly one week later, is connected with the celebration of the feast.

6. Alexander Schmemann, *For the Life of the World* (Crestwood, NY: St. Vladimir's Seminary Press, 1988), p. 58.

5

Major and Minor Festivals and Occasions

The previous chapter explained the overall structure of the church year. The church year can be divided into three parts: the Time of Christmas, the Time of Easter, and the Time of the Church. In addition to this broad outline, the observances of the church can be classified according to the type of festival they are. The following are the types or classes of festivals: Sundays and Major Festivals, Minor Festivals, and Occasions.[1]

The chief day in the church year is *Sunday*. In the early church the first emphasis was on Sunday because it was the weekly celebration of the resurrection of our Lord. Around this day the rest of the liturgical calendar grew. In fact, Sunday can be called "the foundation of the entire structure of the Christian year."[2]

The *Major Festivals* of the church year are the following: the Nativity of Our Lord, the Epiphany of Our Lord, Ash Wednesday, Palm Sunday, Holy Monday, Holy Tuesday, Holy Wednesday, Maundy Thursday, Good Friday, the Resurrection of Our Lord, the Ascension of Our Lord, the Day of Pentecost, and the Holy Trinity. These festivals are called *major* because they "always have precedence over any other day or observance."[3]

The *Minor Festivals* (see fig. 5.1) commemorate the apostles of our Lord, the four evangelists, other great saints and martyrs, and St. Michael the Archangel and All Angels. Included with this group of festivals are three Christological festivals that originated as feasts of the virgin Mary: the Presentation of Our Lord, the Annunciation of Our Lord, and the Visitation. Holy Cross Day, also known as the Triumph of the Cross, originated when the emperor Constantine dedicated a church built over the supposed site of the crucifixion.[4]

Finally, of special significance for Lutheran churches are the observances of the Presentation of the Augsburg Confession and the Reformation.

When a minor festival falls on a Sunday, its Collect of the Day may follow the Collect appointed for that Sunday of the church year. It has become a widespread practice to observe Reformation on the last Sunday in October and All Saints' Day on the first Sunday in November. Unless October 31 falls on a Sunday, this means that Reformation Day is celebrated on the Sunday prior to the festival. If other minor festivals are transferred to a Sunday, ordinarily they are observed on the Sunday after the date.[5]

Finally, there are the *Occasions* (see fig. 5.1): Dedication of a Church, Anniversary of a Congregation, Mission Festival, Harvest Festival, Day of Supplication and Prayer, Day of Special or National Thanksgiving. These occasions may be observed on any day except on major festivals.[6]

Generally speaking, the observance of the major festivals of the church year has been fairly constant. Among the minor festivals the church has held on to those which commemorate the apostles and evangelists. More fluctuation has occurred with the other festivals. It seems that almost every generation in the church makes changes to the liturgical calendar. As James Brauer has stated, "The list of saints' days has never stayed firm for long."[7]

The lesser festivals fall on the same dates every year. There is a problem, however, with most of the Sundays and major festivals because of the variable date for Easter. So that the altar guild members know what Sunday of the church year it is and when the major festivals occur, it is a good idea to have a church calendar which indicates the dates for these occasions each year. Most church calendars also indicate the appropriate liturgical color.[8]

Notes

1. See the outline of the church year in *Lutheran Worship* (St. Louis: Concordia Publishing House, 1982), pp. 8–9.

2. The *New Westminster Dictionary of Liturgy and Worship*, ed. by J. G. Davies (Philadelphia: Westminster Press, 1986), s.v. "Sunday," by R. F. Buxton.

3. *Lutheran Worship Altar Book* (St. Louis: Concordia Publishing House, 1982), p. 12.

4. J. C. J. Metford, *The Christian Year* (London: Thames and Hudson, 1991), p. 85.

5. James Brauer, in *Lutheran Worship: History and Practice* (St. Louis: Concordia Publishing House, 1993), p. 165, rightly points out that "the importance of and the precedence given to Sundays should limit such practice."

6. *Lutheran Worship Altar Book*, p. 12.

7. Brauer, p. 171.

8. Concordia Publishing House produces a "Church Year Calendar" on one sheet which lists all of the Sundays and major festivals with their calendar date, lectionary readings, and appropriate liturgical color.

Figure 5.1 Minor Festivals and Occasions

MINOR FESTIVALS

November
    30 St. Andrew, Apostle*

December
    21 St. Thomas, Apostle
    26 St. Stephen, The First Martyr
    27 St. John, Apostle and Evangelist
    28 The Holy Innocents, Martyrs
    31 New Year's Eve
        Eve of the Name of Jesus

January
    1 New Year's Day
        The Circumcision of Our Lord
    18 The Confession of St. Peter
    24 St. Timothy, Pastor and Confessor
    25 The Conversion of St. Paul
    26 St. Titus, Pastor and Confessor

February
    2 The Presentation of Our Lord
    18 Martin Luther, Doctor and
        Confessor
    24 St. Matthias, Apostle

March
    25 The Annunciation of Our Lord

April
    25 St. Mark, Evangelist

May
    1 St. Philip and St. James, Apostles
    7 C. F. W. Walther, Doctor
    31 The Visitation

June
    11 St. Barnabas, Apostle
    24 The Nativity of St. John the Baptist
    25 Presentation of the Augsburg
        Confession
    29 St. Peter and St. Paul, Apostles

July
    22 St. Mary Magdalene
    25 St. James the Elder, Apostle

August
    10 St. Laurence, Martyr
    15 St. Mary, Mother of Our Lord
    24 St. Bartholomew, Apostle

September
    14 Holy Cross Day
    21 St. Matthew, Apostle and Evangelist
    29 St. Michael and All Angels

October
    18 St. Luke, Evangelist
    28 St. Simon and St. Jude, Apostles
    31 Reformation Day

November
    1 All Saints' Day
    2 Commemoration of the Faithful
        Departed

OCCASIONS

    Dedication of a Church
    Anniversary of a Congregation
    Mission Festival
    Harvest Festival
    Day of Supplication and Prayer
    Day of Special or National
        Thanksgiving

*St. Andrew's Day determines the First Sunday in Advent and therefore begins the enumeration of the minor festivals.

6

Liturgical Colors

The liturgical colors are those colors that are used for paraments, vestments, and accessories such as banners and other decorations. Color is an adjunct to the worship of the church but contributes to the times and seasons of the church year.

The use of color in the church has developed for both psychological and didactic reasons. It is natural to associate certain colors with particular moods, and the mood or tenor of a season of the church year is appropriately conveyed by the use of a particular color. The liturgical colors that will be discussed in this chapter have to do with their evolvement and use in the Western rites of the church. The association of a color with an attitude or state of mind may vary from culture to culture.

In the early church there was no fixed rule for determining the color for a season or festival. Ordinarily the newest and best paraments and vestments were used for the more important occasions. It was not until the 16th century that certain colors were assigned to be used during particular seasons and on certain feast days. Complete standardization of colors was not achieved until the 19th century, and this, as the story goes, was due only to the commercial influence of the ecclesiastical supply houses.[1]

In 1570 with the reformed missal of Pope Pius V the common sequence, called "the Roman use," was established. The high festivals of Christmas and Easter were white. The preparatory seasons of Advent and Lent were purple. The penitential days of Ash Wednesday and Good Friday were black. The days of zeal (Pentecost) and martyrs were red. The other days were green. There is no reason that this usage must be adhered to. The external matter of color falls under the category of *adiaphora* or matters that are neither right nor wrong. But since the Lutheran Church is part of the Western rite, it usually follows the customary liturgical practices.

The following is a list of the standard liturgical colors, describing their significance and use during the church year.

White: The color of purity and eternity, symbolizing perfection, celebration, and joy. White is used for Christmas and its season, Epiphany and its season (usually until the Eve of the Second Sunday after the Epiphany; but see also page 79), and Easter and its season (until the Eve of Pentecost). Also for the Feast of the Holy Trinity and for the Christological festivals of the Annunciation, the Visitation, the Presentation, and the Transfiguration. It is used for St. Michael and All Angels and for the festivals of saints who were not martyrs. If Holy Communion is celebrated on Maundy Thursday, the color is white. White may also be used for a mission festival or a day of special or national thanksgiving.

Red: The color of zeal (fire) and martyrdom (blood). Red is the color of Pentecost, from the Eve of Pentecost until the Eve of the Holy Trinity. It is also used for the festivals of saints who died as martyrs. Red is the color for Reformation. It is also appropriate for Ordination, the Dedication of a Church, and the Anniversary of a Congregation

Green: The color of life, refreshment, and regeneration. Green is used for the season after Pentecost, beginning with the Eve of the Second Sunday after Pentecost. It may also be used for the Epiphany season, from the Eve of the Second Sunday after the Epiphany until the Eve of the Transfiguration.

Purple: The color of royalty, but also of sorrow and repentance. Purple is used during the Advent season (until the Eve of the Nativity) and during the Lenten season (until after the Maundy Thursday service, if Holy Communion is not celebrated). It may also be used on a Day of Supplication and Prayer.

Black: The color of mourning, humility, and death. Black is used on Ash Wednesday (as an alternate) and Good Friday.

The following is a list of optional colors that may be used during certain seasons or on certain days in place of the standard ones described above.

Blue: The color of spiritual love, fidelity, anticipation, and hope. Blue is often used on festivals of St. Mary, the Mother of Our Lord. It is also an alternate color for Advent, because, since the liturgical revisions of the 1960s, the tenor of the season is one of hope and anticipation of the coming of Christ.

Scarlet: The color of royalty and passion. Scarlet is an alternate color for Holy Week, used until after the Maundy Thursday service (if, contrary to Lutheran custom, Holy Communion is not celebrated).

Gold: The color of riches and glory. Gold may be used on Easter Day, the "queen" of festivals, as an alternate to white.

Rose: The color of anticipation and joy. If a congregation observes *Gaudete* or *Laetare*, which in the midst of their preparatory seasons anticipate the joy of Christmas and Easter respectively, rose may be used in place of purple (or blue and purple).

In employing these liturgical colors it is important to note what was said in the previous chapter about Sundays and major and minor festivals. The color for the week is determined by the Sunday, except in the case of Christmas (after Christmas it is no longer Advent but the Christmas season, during which the color white is used). If a minor festival falls during the week and is observed, the color for that festival is used, but after its observance the color for the week is restored. If a minor festival is transferred to a Sunday and is observed, the color of the minor festival may be used on that Sunday, although the precedence of Sundays should make such an observance an exception rather than a rule. Ordinarily, the transference of a minor festival should not be done during the Time of Christmas or the Time of Easter. The three minor festivals most commonly transferred to Sunday are the following: St. Michael and All Angels on the Sunday after September 29, Reformation Day on the Sunday before October 31, and All Saints' Day on the Sunday after November 1. If any of these festivals falls on a Sunday, it may be observed on that Sunday.

It is also important to note that, in employing liturgical colors, it is the season of the church year that determines their use. This means that the color of the day or season is not changed for wedding or funeral services. The only exceptions are for services of ordination, church dedication, and congregational anniversary, in which cases red is the appropriate color.

Notes

1. See *The New Westminster Dictionary of Liturgy and Worship*, ed. by J. G. Davies (Philadelphia: Westminster Press, 1986), s.v. "Colours, Liturgical," by Gilbert Cope.

PART III

7

Sacred Space

The church in its primary sense is "the assembly of all believers among whom the Gospel is preached in its purity and the holy Sacraments are administered according to the Gospel."[1] This means that, above all other things, the church is people, *believers,* who hear the Gospel and use the Sacraments according to Christ's institution. With this understanding it is possible to say that it does not make any difference where these believers hear the Gospel and use the Sacraments, whether it be in a traditional church building, a gymnasium, or even a storefront. During the first few centuries of the church's existence Christians, for various reasons, met in the homes of believers. What was, and is, important is not so much where they met but the activity that was going on when they met.

On the other hand, the place where believers meet is important. After all, the church is also the *assembly* of people who hear the Gospel and use the Sacraments. Those people must assemble somewhere, and the character and purpose of their assembly require that the place of the assembly be appropriate for what is going on. It would not seem appropriate to serve a formal dinner with china and crystal on a picnic table. Likewise, the place where God's Word is heard and the Sacraments received should be in a setting that is conducive to that hearing and receiving and does not detract from it in any way.

The most important reason, however, for being concerned about where God's people are gathered is not because the nature of worship is corporate but because it is sacramental. Where the Gospel is rightly preached and the Sacraments administered according to Christ's institution, there God has promised to be. This means that the place of worship is not just symbolic of God's presence but is the place where he is really present. Where God is present demands the utmost of respect and reverence, as Moses experienced in the wilderness: "Take off your sandals, for the place where you are standing is holy ground" (Exodus 3:5). Accordingly, our churches today need to be shown that respect and, in turn, further that spirit of reverence. As one writer put it, "Well-appointed worship space helps thoughtful worshipers reflect and say, 'We have been in the house of God today.' "[2]

It is necessary for the members of the altar guild to know these principles of worship and sacred space so that they may carry out their duties with the appropriate reverence and devotion. It is also important for them to be familiar with the terms used to designate the different parts of the worship space. The two main divisions of the worship space are the *chancel* and the *nave*.

Before we continue, a word must be said about the orientation of a church building. In the early church the building was constructed so that the altar was at the east end. This tradition is not always followed today, but the terminology for designating the parts of the building remains in use. The front (or altar) end of the building is called its liturgical *east*, the back its liturgical *west*. As one faces the front, the left is liturgical *north* (also called the *Gospel side*) and the right is liturgical *south* (also called the *Epistle side*).

The *nave* is the large area of the worship space where the congregation is gathered. (The word *nave* comes from the Latin *navis*, which means "ship," an early symbol for the church.) In traditionally constructed churches the nave is a rectangle, with the longer dimension extending from front to back (see fig. 7.1). It has two rows of pews (from front to back) with a main, center aisle and two side aisles. In some churches the nave is almost square and the pews are situated in a semicircular orientation to the altar. The nave in this style of church may have additional aisles radiating from the chancel.

It should be noted that many modern church buildings (and some renovated naves) do not have pews. Instead chairs are used which can be arranged and/or removed depending on how the congregation utilizes the worship space. An advantage of chairs over pews is that the seating in the nave can be arranged to accommodate certain types of services. The removal of chairs would permit the nave to be used for a purpose other than worship. However, the use of the nave for an activity other than worship seems to be incompatible with the idea that this particular space has been set aside for sacred use. It would also preclude the use of the church as a place for individual prayer and devotion outside of the appointed service time.

The *chancel* is the second main division of sacred space. It is on the liturgical east of the building where the altar is located (see fig. 7.1). (The term *chancel* is derived from the Latin *cancelli*, which means "lattices" or "crossbars," which originally separated the nave from the altar area.) In most churches the chancel is set off from the nave by being on a level one or two steps above the floor of the nave. The altar itself sits on a platform called a *predella* or *footpace*, which is at least one step higher than the surrounding area (see fig. 8.1). The chancel, in turn, can be divided into two parts. The west end (closest to the nave) is called the *choir*, because the singers who assisted with the liturgy sat there. The east end of the chancel is called the *sanctuary*, the area immediately around the altar.[3] Sometimes the sanctuary and choir are separated by a low rail referred to as either an *altar rail* or *communion rail*.

At the liturgical west of the church building is the *narthex*. This room serves as the entryway leading from the outside of the building into the nave (see fig. 7.1). As the entryway it marks the passage from the outside world to the presence of God. Its appointments and decoration should help to facilitate that passage. The narthex also serves as a gathering place for processions on festival days and at weddings and funerals. In some churches the baptismal font is located in the narthex, a practice originating in the medieval period to signify that Baptism is the means by which a person "enters" the Christian assembly.

In some churches, where the nave and chancel adjoin, there are extensions to the liturgical north (left) and south (right). These extensions are called *transepts*. If viewed from above, the floor space of the church would be cruciform or cross-shaped (see fig. 7.1). Occasionally, however, a church building may have only one transept. Frequently the transepts contain pews or chairs for additional seating. Sometimes the baptismal font is located in one of the transepts, in which case that transept would be called a *baptistery*.

Since about the fifth century a church building has also had a room called a *sacristy*, where the sacred utensils and vestments were kept. Generally the sacristy is located immediately to the side or rear of the chancel. In some churches there may be two types of sacristies. The *clergy sacristy* (which is **not** an office) is where the vestments are kept and where the minister prepares for the service. Another name for this sacristy is the term *vestry*.

The other sacristy is called the *working* or *altar guild sacristy*. This is where the paraments, linens, sacred vessels, candles, and other liturgical appointments are kept. At a very minimum there should be a closet and cupboard space so that these appointments can be stored neatly and be kept free from damage, and a sink so that the sacred vessels can be washed after use. A more elaborate working sacristy may have a large working table, facilities for laundering and ironing linens and paraments, cleaning supplies and equipment, a piscina for disposing of consecrated wine and baptismal water, and the like. In instances where there is only one sacristy for minister and altar guild, the members of the altar guild should have their work done ahead of time so that they do not disturb the minister's preparation for the service.

The duties of the altar guild with respect to the church building as a whole will vary from place to place. Traditionally, members of this group were responsible for the entire place of worship. That practice is still a good one to follow because the entire worship space is the setting for the Divine Service. A Christian congregation needs a group of people to care for the place of worship and to prepare for its services so that God may be glorified and the worshipers edified.

Notes

1. Augsburg Confession, Article VII. From *The Book of Concord*, translated and edited by Theodore G. Tappert (Philadelphia: Fortress Press, 1959), p. 32.

2. Wayne Schmidt, "The Place of Worship," in *Lutheran Worship: History and Practice*, edited by Fred L. Precht (St. Louis: Concordia Publishing House, 1993), p. 219.

3. The term *sanctuary* is sometimes used to refer to the whole worship space, namely, the nave and chancel together. Some purists regard this use as improper and insist that the word be applied only to the east end of the chancel where the altar is located.

Figure 7.1 Church floor plans, traditional and modern

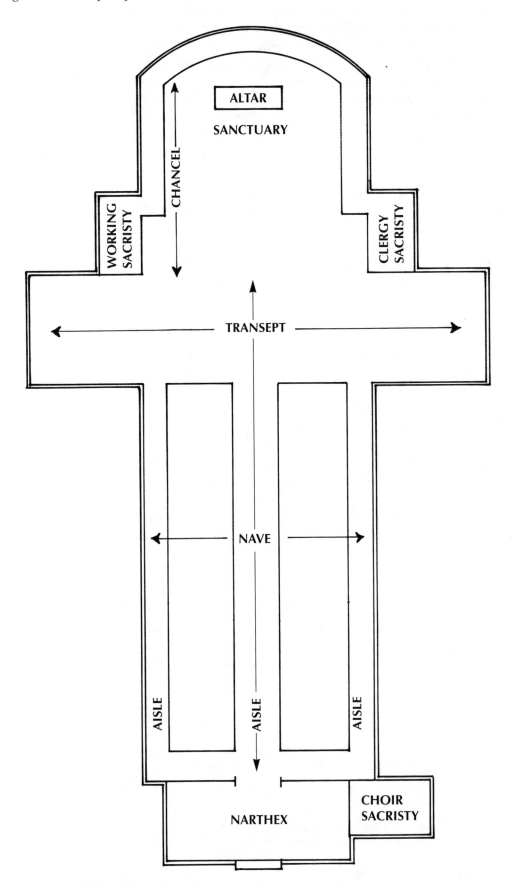

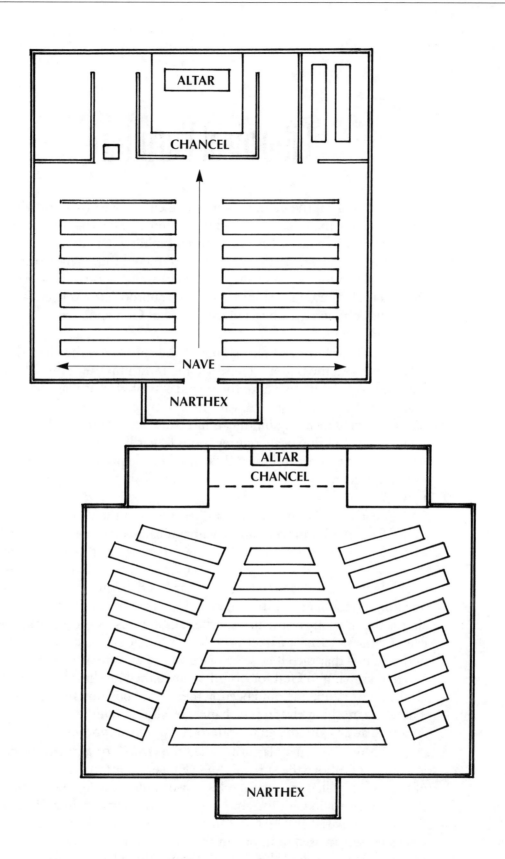

8

Liturgical Furniture

The furnishings of the nave, which can be either pews (with or without kneelers) or chairs, were described in chapter 7. This chapter concerns the furniture of the chancel. Like the church building itself, these furnishings can be discussed from a utilitarian viewpoint, and they can be simple or ornate. From a theological viewpoint, since they concern the sacred acts of the church, these furnishings should be appropriate for what is going on and be conducive for hearing the Word of God and receiving his gifts in the Sacraments.

The major liturgical furnishings in the church are the altar, the baptismal font, and the pulpit.[1] These are the most important furnishings because it is from them where the sacred acts of liturgical action are done. The style of this furniture will vary from simple to ornate, from traditional to modern, depending on the architectural style of the building and the circumstances of the local congregation. Regardless of their style, however, the altar, the font, and the pulpit should be kept immaculately clean and in mint condition in accordance with their function as places of sacred activity.

The *altar* is the focal point of the services of the church. The term comes from the Latin word *altare* which means the place or structure where a sacrifice is offered.[2] In Lutheran theology this sacrifice is understood to be the great sacrifice of Jesus Christ for the salvation of the world. With that understanding the altar has two important symbolic functions: sacramental and sacrificial. The sacramental function of the altar is that it is one of the places where God gives us the gifts that result from Christ's sacrifice, namely, the Lord's Supper. The sacrificial purpose of the altar is that the altar is the place where we offer our prayer, praise, and thanksgiving to God for his gifts. Since the altar has this great role in Christian worship, it should occupy the central position in the chancel. Therefore, nothing else in the chancel or church building should take our attention away from the altar or detract from its importance.

The altar sits on a platform called the *predella* or *footpace*, which is at least one step above the surrounding chancel floor (see fig. 8.1). The top of the altar is called the *mensa*, a Latin word meaning "table." The use of this term has to do with the altar being the place from which the Lord's Supper is prepared and served. On traditional altars the mensa has five Greek crosses incised in it, one in the center and one at each of the four corners.[3] At the back of the altar (if it is positioned against the east wall) there is a *gradine* or *retable*. Properly, the gradine is a shelf on which the candlesticks sit. Occasionally, it has been called a candlebench as well. On the gradine there is invariably also placed, according to Lutheran custom, a crucifix, which is preferred over an altar cross. For some large altars there may be more than one gradine.

In most Lutheran churches in this country that were constructed before the 1960s, the altar was usually positioned against the *east* wall of the chancel. It has become more common since then to plan the chancel so that a *freestanding altar* can be built. This change has resulted from renewed attention to a recommendation made by Dr. Martin Luther: "In the true Mass, however, of real Christians, the altar should not remain where it is [that is, against the wall], and the priest should always face the people as Christ undoubtedly did in the Last Supper."[4] A good case, theologically and historically, can be made for a freestanding altar. Even churches that presently have an altar fixed to the east wall may be renovated in most cases to accommodate a freestanding one.

Figure 8.1 Altar, showing parts and location, and credence

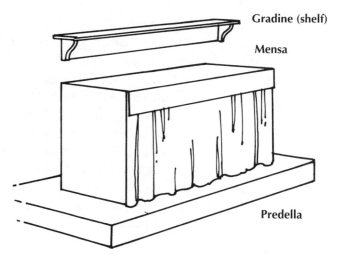

Gradine (shelf)

Mensa

Predella

Fixed and freestanding altars

The second major piece of liturgical furniture in the church is the *baptismal font*. The word font (not *fount*) is derived from the Latin *fons*, meaning "spring" or "fountain." Unlike the altar, the location of the font in the worship space has varied quite a bit. In the medieval period and in some modern churches the font is located in the narthex. This practice intended to symbolize that Holy Baptism was the means by which a person enters the Christian community. An ancient practice that has persisted throughout the history of the church is to locate the font in a room or building separate from the main worship space. In this case the room or building is called a *baptistery* or *baptistry*. In some churches one of the transepts of the nave serves as the baptistery.

The more common practice in Lutheran churches has been for the font to stand near or in the chancel (see fig. 8.2). Positioned between the chancel and the nave, the font can stand in the areas to the left or right of the chancel or even in the center. Being in or near the chancel, the font is more closely associated with the other two major liturgical furnishings, the altar and the pulpit. In some

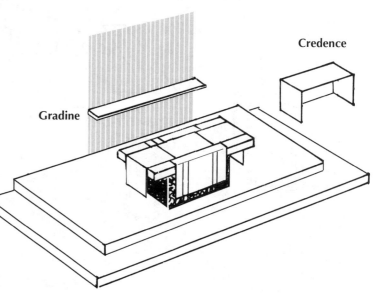

Credence

Gradine

churches the font is "portable," that is, not permanently fixed to the floor. To be avoided with the moveable font is pushing it off into a corner when not in use. The font should remain in a location that is commensurate with its place in Lutheran theology. Another caveat is to avoid positioning the font so that it interferes with the prominence of the altar.

The third major piece of liturgical furniture is the *pulpit* (see fig. 8.2), also sometimes called *ambo*. The word *pulpit* comes from the Latin *pulpitum*, which means "scaffold" or "stage." A medieval invention, the pulpit is a podium that was elevated so that the speaker could better project his voice. In larger churches it worked out better acoustically to locate the pulpit about a third or half of the way into the nave, either attaching it to one of the massive columns holding the roof up or positioning it against one of the side walls. Modern audio systems have made that feature unnecessary today. Nevertheless, the pulpit is still raised above the nave (and chancel) floor. This elevation allows for all those listening to see the speaker, but more important it signifies the prominence of the proclamation of the Word of God.

As stated previously, the three major liturgical furnishings should be kept clean and in an unblemished condition. In this regard the pulpit and font fare usually well. Not so fortunate is the altar, which can easily assume a sloppy appearance. The only items that should be found on the altar are the appointments intended for it (treated in chapter 9). The mensa is not a shelf for empty offering plates, extra hymnals, bulletins, and service notes. These and other such items create a cluttered appearance and detract from the dignity and prominence of the altar as a focal point in the service.

Figure 8.2 Font and pulpit,
showing location, and lectern

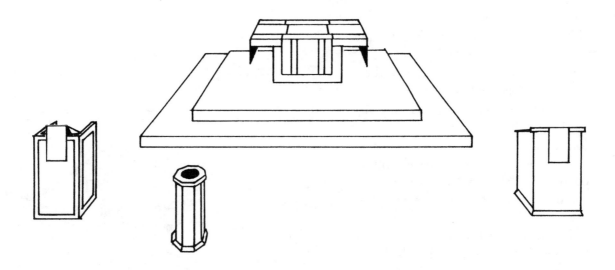

In addition to the altar, the font, and the pulpit there are other liturgical furnishings that may be found in the worship space. In most Lutheran churches there is also a *lectern* (from the Latin *lectio*, "reading"). Usually the lectern is on the same line dividing the chancel from the nave as the pulpit and is located at the side of the chancel opposite the pulpit (see fig. 8.2). Normally smaller than the pulpit, the lectern serves as the place from where the Scriptures are read.

Also common in many Lutheran churches is the *altar rail*, also called a *communion* or *chancel rail*. This rail divides the chancel into the sanctuary and the choir or, less commonly, divides the chancel from the nave (see fig. 8.3). In small chancels the rail extends from the liturgical north to the south walls, often having a gate in the middle which closes off the sanctuary from the choir. In a larger chancel there may be rails on three or even all four sides of the sanctuary. In this arrangement there are ordinarily no gates.

Historically, the use of the altar rail arose during the Middle Ages with the separation of the clergy from the laity and a changing theology of the Sacrament of the Altar. Practically, however, the rail provided a place for people to kneel to receive the Sacrament.[5] In addition to being a place to receive the Sacrament, the rail is also used as a place to kneel for absolution, confirmation, and holy matrimony.

Another piece of liturgical furniture is the *credence*, which can be either a *credence table* or a *credence shelf*. Usually located on the south wall of the chancel, the credence holds the vessels containing the elements to be used for the Lord's Supper (see fig. 8.1). These vessels are brought to the altar during the offertory. The credence may also hold a lavabo, an oil stock or cruet, or the incense boat. If all these appointments are used, a second credence should be installed on the other chancel wall to avoid a cluttered appearance.

Most Lutheran chancels contain *sedilia* (from the Latin *sedile*, "seat"), which are the chairs or benches for the pastor and any assistants that he may have. These seats are located on the liturgical north and south walls of the chancel, usually in the choir section of the chancel (see fig. 8.3). In front of the sedile there is sometimes a *prie dieu* (from the French, literally "pray God") or kneeling desk. This desk is an individual kneeler that has a shelf to hold books.

Behind the altar, whether fixed or freestanding, there may be a decorative panel or screen called a *reredos* (see fig. 8.4). The reredos may be stone or wood, depending on what material the altar is made of. This panel may contain a niche for a crucifix or statue. For an altar that is fixed against the east wall, the reredos, gradine, and altar are usually constructed as one piece, and the reredos itself may not extend all the way to the floor but simply rest on the top of the back of the altar. With a freestanding altar, the reredos, with or without a gradine, extends all the way to the floor. Instead of a niche or carving, a reredos may also be decorated with a tapestry or painting. If there are side panels which close to cover the painting or other decoration, the reredos is properly called a *triptych*.

Instead of a reredos, the altar may have a *dossal* or *dorsal* (see fig. 8.4). The dossal is an ornamental cloth hung behind the altar from a rod. Sometimes the dossal fabric is such that it coordinates with all the parament colors, sometimes the dossal color matches that of the paraments. In the latter instance, the dossal fabric should be the same as the parament fabric. If the dossal extends at right angles on either side of the altar, these extensions are called *riddels*, which are suspended on rods mounted on *riddel posts*. Aesthetically, riddels provide an enclosure for the altar; practically, they restrict drafts which are common in large buildings.[6]

As with the altar, font, and pulpit, extreme care should be exercised in maintaining these other liturgical furnishings. They should be regularly cleaned and refurbished or replaced so that the chancel does not have a run-down appearance. Also, if installing furnishings in addition to the altar, font, and pulpit, care should be taken so that any added piece of furniture harmonizes with what is already there and does not result in a cluttered appearance.

Figure 8.3 Altar rail and sedilia

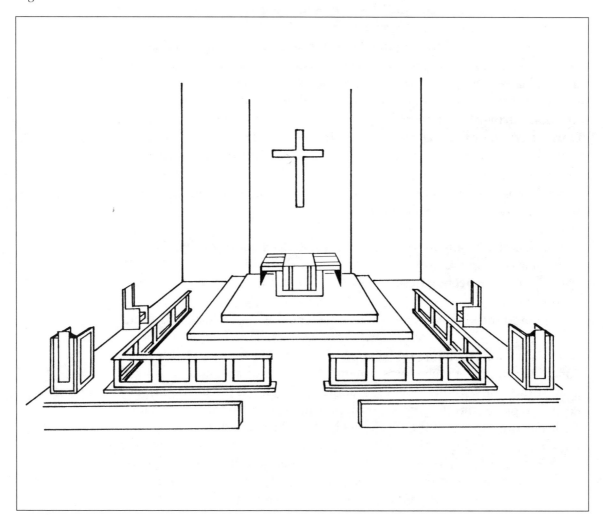

Figure 8.4 Reredos, dossal

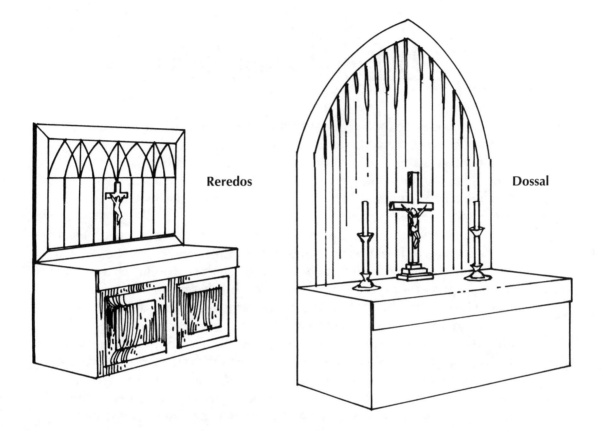

Reredos

Dossal

Notes

1. See Wayne E. Schmidt, "The Place of Worship," in *Lutheran History: Worship and Practice*, edited by Fred L. Precht (St. Louis: Concordia Publishing House, 1993), pp. 196–211, for a more extensive theological and historical discussion of these furnishings.

2. *The New Westminster Dictionary of Liturgy and Worship*, ed. by J. G. Davies (Philadelphia: Westminster Press, 1986), s.v. "Altar," by C. E. Pocknee.

3. Paul H. D. Lang, *What an Altar Guild Should Know* (St. Louis: Concordia Publishing House, 1964), p. 52.

4. *The German Mass and Order of Service, 1526*, in *Luther's Works, American Edition*, vol. 53, p. 69.

5. This was a practice that also arose in the medieval period, probably as a result of a spirit of both veneration and fear on the part of the laity that accompanied the changing sacramental theology. Up to that time the practice was to receive the Sacrament while standing. This practice has been the rule in the Eastern Orthodox churches and has been revived in recent years in western (including Lutheran) churches.

6. For further information on the size and construction of dossals and riddels, see Lang, p. 57.

9

Liturgical Appointments

The accessories or appointments in the sacred space, which will be found primarily in the chancel, vary in number and elaborateness. Besides the paraments (discussed below in Part IV) and sacred vessels (Part V), there should be, at a minimum, a cross or crucifix, the service book, a stand for this book, and candles. Additional appointments may be used as the season or local custom permits.

The most important appointment in the chancel is the *cross* or *crucifix*. According to Pocknee and Randall, the history and use of the cross or crucifix in worship is long and complicated.[1] In the early church a cross, usually a processional cross, was placed in a bracket or socket next to the altar. During the Middle Ages the custom arose of placing a cross on the altar or gradine, but this practice did not become very widespread until after the Reformation. A corollary development occurred with the use of the crucifix. Again, in the early church a plain cross was used. The crucifix, a cross with the body of the suffering Christ on it, began to appear in the late medieval period when there was an increasing emphasis on the Passion of Christ. From a Lutheran perspective, however, the use of the crucifix has much to commend it.[2]

Despite its late invention, the altar cross is extremely common in Lutheran churches. It sits at the back of the mensa or on the gradine (see fig. 9.1). With a freestanding altar it should be placed on the gradine attached to the reredos, if there is one; if placed on the freestanding altar itself it would be an obstruction between the presiding minister and the congregation. There are, however, other methods for placing a cross or crucifix in the chancel. One way is to affix it to the liturgical east wall behind the altar. If there is a reredos or dossal on this wall, the ceiling should be high enough so that the cross does not make the wall look crowded. It is also possible, if the cross harmonizes with the reredos, to affix it directly on the reredos (this placement would obviously not work on a dossal). Another method is to suspend the cross from the ceiling. A suspended cross should be directly over or slightly behind the altar, in either case centered over the altar on its north/south axis (see fig. 9.2). A third way is to attach a cross to the front of the altar or to have it carved in the wood or stone of the altar. This placement works better if the altar is freestanding and higher above the floor than normal. Finally, the ancient practice of placing a processional cross into a socket next to the altar could be restored.

Regardless of the type or placement of the cross, it should be made of a high quality material and large enough so that it can be clearly seen from any place in the worship space. Something that should be avoided in placing a cross on the altar or in the chancel is the proliferation of crosses in the chancel area. More is not always better, and the multiplication of this emblem lessens the impact and devotional character that an individual cross of beauty and prominence conveys.

Several books are necessary for conducting the services: the altar book or missal (from the Latin *missa*, "mass"; a term originating in the medieval period for the book containing what was said or sung at the Mass or Divine Service), the agenda, the lectionary, and hymnals for the pastor and any assistants. The *altar book* contains the liturgy of the chief service, the offices for morning and evening prayer, the complete psalter, and all of the propers. This book is placed on the altar on the *missal stand*. If the missal stand is metal, a piece of cloth should be placed on it before setting the altar book on the stand in order to protect the leather of the book.

The placement of the missal stand (and book) on the altar will vary. For the chief service the communion vessels should be in the center of the altar. Accordingly, the missal stand should be placed to the left or right of the corporal, at an angle so that it can be read easily by the presiding minister. For the offices (unless, as more customary, they are conducted from the sedilia), the missal stand may be placed at the center of the altar. In this instance, the top and bottom edge of the stand should be parallel to the edges of the mensa. Both of the above arrangements work on both fixed and freestanding altars. It should be noted that for an office, however, since its liturgy is almost entirely sacrificial (prayer and praise), the missal stand should be placed so that the officiant can conduct the service from in front of the freestanding altar. For the benediction he may step behind the altar or simply turn and face the people.

The second book needed for the conduct of the services is the *agenda*. Basically, the agenda contains the occasional rites and services (Baptism, confirmation, marriage, funeral), rites for ordaining/commissioning and installing church workers, and the special liturgies and lectionary for the Lenten season. Many times the pastor will use this book outside of the chancel (for example, on home visitation, at the hospital, or at the cemetery). When the agenda is used in a service, it will ordinarily be held by the presiding or assisting minister.

Many congregations also use a *lectionary*, which is a book containing the Scripture readings for Sundays, major and minor festivals, and the occasions. Some lectionaries also contain psalms, introits, graduals, and offertory verses. With the use of printed lessons for hearers to follow and the profusion of Bible versions that are read from, it has become common in some places to read the appointed Scripture readings from a sheet of paper. While the important thing is the Word of God that is being read, the book from which it is read should be both large and splendid in order to reflect the significance that the Word of God has in Lutheran theology. This principle is especially important to observe if carrying the book in an entrance or Gospel procession or if the readings are read from the altar (where the book is held in the hands).

The final book needed for services is, of course, the *hymnal*. The hymnal is the service book of the people. Along with the Bible and the Catechism, it is a book that every Christian should own. In the hymnal the liturgy is printed to assist the congregation in following and learning it (compare the altar book, which is printed to facilitate the ministers' parts). The other part of the hymnal contains the hymns of the church. For this reason, hymnals are needed in the chancel for the pastor and any assistants, since they should participate in the singing of the hymns. In recent years it has become popular to print the liturgy and hymns in the service folder so that the use of the hymnal is unnecessary. While this practice may facilitate participation of those who are unfamiliar with Lutheran worship, it does the people of God a disservice in the long run. It robs them of the opportunity to learn and know the hymnal not only as a book for the services of the church but also as a devotional book for use in the home. A little effort in catechesis may help restore the hymnal as a church and home book.

A final word that needs to be said about the service books is the matter of color. Several colors are usually available, but the choice of color should be made in consideration of what fits best with the decor of the church. Moreover, at least in the chancel, all of the service books should be of the same color. A black altar book, a red agenda, a blue lectionary, and a green hymnal give the appearance of being a hodgepodge collection. To have all the chancel service books be only one color is more aesthetically pleasing and contributes to the dignified appearance that the chancel should have.

The use of *candles* in the church, like that of crosses, has a long and varied history. In the early church oil lamps were most likely used, with candles becoming more popular later on (apparently in the fourth century). Also, candles (or lamps) were not set directly on the altar at first. Like the cross, lights were set in stands near the altar or sometimes held by assistants (see fig. 9.2). The practice of placing candlesticks directly on the altar appears to have arisen in the 12th century.[3] One of the primary uses of lights, until the invention of the light bulb, was practical: so that people could see in the dark. But the symbolic use of lights, a symbolism that has its roots in the Old Testament (already in Genesis 1:3), is also important. The most basic Christian symbolism attached to the use of lights is derived from the statement of Jesus: "I am the Light of the world" (John 8:12).

The most common symbolic and ceremonial light in the church is the candle. Care should be exercised in purchasing candles. Most liturgical experts recommend that they be at least 51% beeswax. Other candles, such as the type made with stearine, may be cheaper, but beeswax candles burn longer and cleaner. Candle *followers* also help candles to burn longer and cleaner by preventing dripping and uneven burning. A few liturgical purists argue against using them, but there is neither a liturgical or aesthetical reason not to. If followers are used, however, they should be made from the same material as the candleholder.

Other types of lights have been promoted by ecclesiastical supply companies, such as electric candles and tubes made to look like candles with a spring inside to push the candles upward as they burn shorter. The reason put forward against using these devices is that they are artificial. A different device that may have some merit, however, is the oil-burning candle. Burning oil for light predates the invention and use of wax candles, so at least there is historical (and biblical) precedent for this type of light. The contention that oil-burning candles are devised to look like wax candles and not oil lamps may be a valid reason against using them, but the ancient practice of burning oil in a sacred place offers a good balance to that argument.

The number and arrangement of candles in the chancel has varied greatly in the history of the church. The use of candles on the altar, as mentioned above, is of medieval origin. Today most churches have at least two candles on the altar. These candles are called *eucharistic lights* because they usually burn only for the service of the Eucharist or Holy Communion. Liturgiologists are divided on whether they should be lighted for noncommunion services. Since lights are symbolic of God and Jesus Christ as the Light of the world, however, there is no good reason to forbid using them at other services.

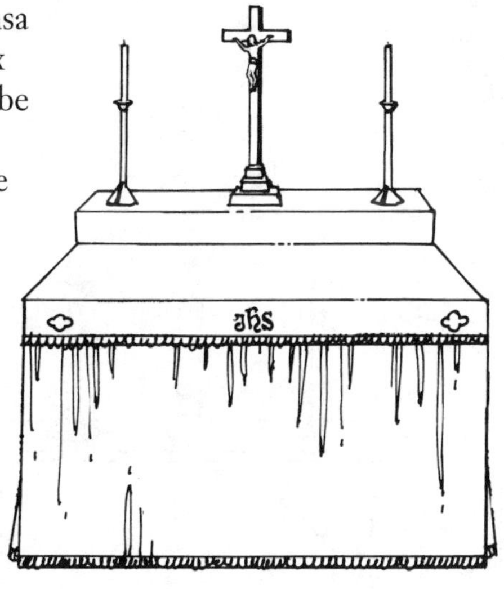

Figure 9.1 Fixed altar, traditional, crucifix on gradine, two eucharistic lights on gradine

The placement of the eucharistic lights depends on the type of altar in the chancel. With a freestanding altar these candles are placed on the liturgical north and south ends of the altar. With a fixed altar the candles may sit on either the back of the mensa or the gradine (see fig. 9.1). If an altar cross or crucifix stands on the altar, the tops of the candles should not be higher than the horizontal beams of the cross. Some modern, freestanding altars are constructed so that the eucharistic lights are mounted on standards which are positioned on the north and south ends of the altar (see fig. 9.2). Like the placement of the cross, this is a practice that was common before the custom arose of putting candlesticks on the altar.

Candelabra (singular *candelabrum*) which hold three, five, or seven candles are sometimes referred to as *office lights*, since they were lighted for the office (noncommunion, prayer) services (see fig. 9.3). Usually they are placed on standards that sit on the floor at the liturgical north and south ends of the altar. With freestanding altars, office lights, mounted on floor standards, should be set back toward the east wall so as not to impede movement around the altar. With a freestanding altar (or a fixed altar, for that matter) office lights might be mounted on the east wall.

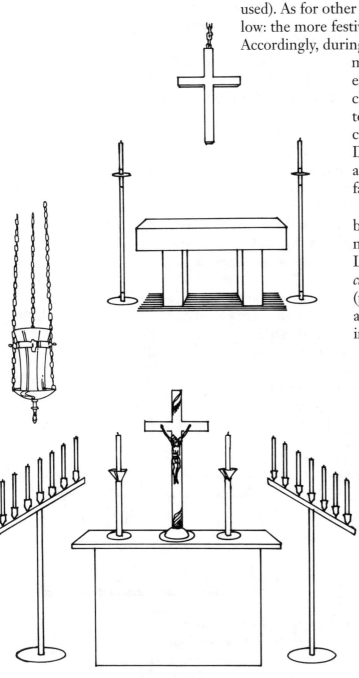

Figure 9.2 Free standing altar, cross suspended from ceiling, two lights in sockets at each end of the altar

How many candles should be used in the chancel? First of all, regarding eucharistic candles, restricting the number to two is better supported in Lutheran tradition than the post-Reformation Roman norm of six. Regrettably, one occasionally sees six eucharistic lights in Lutheran churches, and that at the very time when numerous Roman Catholic altars are returning to two. (Since Vatican II [1962–65], at least two, but even four, six, or, if the bishop of the diocese celebrates, seven candles may be used). As for other lights/candles, a good principle to follow: the more festive the celebration, the more light. Accordingly, during the penitential season of Lent the minimum of lights should be employed. On major festivals of the church year the maximum (according to the equipment on hand and, of course, good taste) could be used. During the "ordinary" times balance and variety might be the determining factor.

In addition to the crucifix, service books, and altar candles other appointments may be used. Common in many Lutheran churches is the *processional cross*. A processional cross is a cross (preferably a crucifix) mounted on a staff and carried (see fig. 9.4). As the name implies, this cross is used in processions. It may be carried in an entrance procession at the beginning of the service, the Gospel procession (when the minister and attendants carry the lectionary or Gospel book into the middle of the nave for reading the Gospel), or, if customary, to the grave site in the service for the Burial of the Dead. When it is not being carried during the service, the processional cross rests in a stand in the chancel or in a bracket mounted on the chancel wall. If a service is being conducted in which there are no processions, the preferred custom is for the processional cross to be placed in the sacristy (unless, of course, the processional cross also serves as the altar or chancel cross).

Figure 9.3 Floor candelabra, candelabra for setting on altar, sanctuary light

Generally used with the processional cross are *processional torches*. These torches are candles mounted on staves which match the staff of the processional cross (see fig. 9.4). Usually two processional torches are used. In entrance processions they follow the processional cross. In the Gospel procession they also follow the cross but, if the aisle of the nave is wide enough, flank the book from which the Gospel is read.

Frequently seen in a Lutheran church is the *sanctuary light*, sometimes called an *eternal light* (see fig. 9.3). This lamp or candle, hanging from the ceiling or mounted on a wall bracket, burns continuously throughout the year.[4] Some traditions, including many Lutheran, understand the sanctuary light to symbolize the continual presence of God, hence the name eternal light. Concerning the color of the glass of the sanctuary light, some insist that white or untinted glass is to be preferred. Most lamps today, however, have red colored glass, but there is no real reason to make an issue of this matter.

Also becoming more common in Lutheran churches is the use of the *thurible* or *censer* (see fig. 9.4). In the Bible, incense symbolizes the prayers of the faithful rising up before God (Psalm 141:2), as well as the presence of God himself (Isaiah 6). It is especially appropriate for Vespers and Evening Prayer (the verse from Psalm 141 is used in both of these offices). In the Divine Service the traditional moments of using incense are the following: during the Introit, the altar, the ministers, and the people are censed; in the Gospel procession the thurifer (the assistant carrying the thurible) follows the processional cross ahead of the torchbearers; during the singing of the Sanctus the sacred vessels are censed. When not in use the thurible may hang from a bracket mounted on the chancel wall. Necessary to use with the thurible is the *incense boat*, a small bowl or pan which holds the supply of incense to be burned.

Many churches today use *banners*. Banners may be used as an added expression of a festival or season of the church year. Consequently, the banner maker will employ colors, symbols, or words appropriate to that festival or season. In general, banners should symbolize, more than state in words. Normally banners are used in processions; when not in use they may hang in the church from rods attached to the wall or a floor standard, or they may be stored in the sacristy. As with the other appointments, only banners that are works of fine craftsmanship should be used.

A word must also be said about *flags*. Many Lutheran churches display flags in the chancel or nave, but this practice must be discouraged. The national flag is a symbol of the state whose values and purposes are different from, and sometimes incompatible with, those of the church. The "Christian flag"

Figure 9.4
Processional cross, torches, thurible

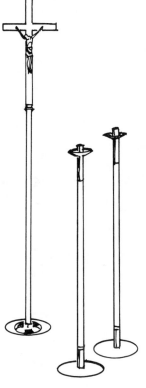

Figure 9.5 Advent wreath

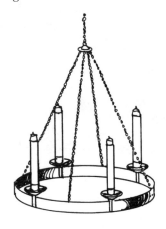

Figure 9.6 Paschal candle

is a piece of redundant and distracting symbolism, since the focus in the church is on the altar and cross in the chancel. Moreover, these flags serve no liturgical function but were introduced into churches for political reasons. If congregations insist on having them, they should be displayed in the narthex or fellowship hall.

In addition to the regular appointments for the chancel and nave, a congregation may choose to use seasonal appointments. One such appointment is the *Advent wreath*, originally used in the home to count the weeks of Advent. The Advent wreath is a circle of evergreen branches with four candles (one lighted for the first week in Advent, two for the second week, and so on). In a horizontal position it may be mounted on a stand or hang from the ceiling (see fig. 9.5). Some Advent wreaths are positioned vertically and hang on the chancel or nave wall. Formerly it was said that the wreath's four candles should be white, but ecclesiastical supply houses have promoted the custom of using colored candles. If the church's Advent paraments are blue, blue candles should be used; if purple paraments, purple candles. With the use of *The Lutheran Hymnal* (1941), when a congregation observed *Gaudete* ("Rejoice"), the Third Sunday in Advent, a rose or pink candle was lighted in the Advent wreath on this day.[5] The use of the "Christ Candle," also promoted by the supply houses, is definitely to be discouraged. First, because it is an importation of the idea of the paschal candle. Secondly, because the Advent wreath belongs to the season preparatory for Christmas, and on the festival of our Savior's birth the wreath should be removed from the church.

Another seasonal appointment is the *paschal candle* (see fig. 9.6). The paschal (from the Greek *pascha* meaning "Easter") candle symbolizes the resurrection victory over the darkness of sin and death. The use of this candle goes back to the early church (fourth or fifth century). The Vigil of Easter marks the first lighting of the paschal candle. In some traditions it is burned until Ascension Day, in others until Pentecost. In the Vigil service it may be carried in procession and placed in a special stand (traditionally to the liturgical north or left of the altar). It remains there for the duration of its use during the Easter season.

On the other hand, the paschal candle is not just a seasonal appointment. After its use in the chancel during the Easter season, it may be placed next to the baptismal font. Because of the connection between Easter and

Baptism (Romans 6), congregations are encouraged to light the paschal candle for the Sacrament of Holy Baptism. The symbolism of Christ's triumph over death and the grave also makes the use of the paschal candle appropriate for the rite of Christian burial.

There are other appointments or accessories that could be discussed in this chapter. The ecclesiastical supply catalogs are full of products to buy. The following principles should guide a congregation's purchase and use of appointments in the chancel and nave: (1) They should not conflict with the theology of Scripture or the Lutheran Confessions. (2) They should serve a liturgical purpose. (3) Their symbolism or significance should be clear (this matter may involve some instruction by the pastor or altar guild). (4) Avoid clutter, sensationalism, and sentimentalism.

Notes

1. *The New Westminster Dictionary of Liturgy and Worship*, ed. by J. G. Davies (Philadelphia: Westminster Press, 1986), s.v. "Cross, Crucifix," by C. E. Pocknee and D. W. Randall.

2. See Lang's comment on this subject (p. 52): "The crucifix emphasizes the incarnation of Christ and His atoning sacrifice. A plain or empty cross lacks this emphasis. Some say that the plain cross stands for the Resurrection. Be that as it may, it can also represent a devaluation of the Incarnation and a spiritualizing of Christ. The Lutheran Church, however, believes that 'apart from this man there is not God.' " As Lang goes on to point out, however, the use of the crucifix is not necessarily a confessional matter; if it is not, the altar guild should not make an issue of it.

3. For a more detailed history of the use of lights in the church, see *The New Westminster Dictionary of Liturgy and Worship*, ed. by J. G. Davies (Philadelphia: Westminster Press, 1986), s.v. "Candles, Lamps and Lights," by C. E. Pocknee and D. W. Randall.

4. Exceptions are for the period between Good Friday at 3:00 in the afternoon (the traditional hour of the Lord's death) and the Vigil of Easter. During this time the sanctuary light should be extinguished or removed to the sacristy. It is relighted or returned to the chancel during the Vigil's Service of Light.

5. Similarly, the observance of *Laetare* ("Rejoice"), the Fourth Sunday in Lent, was generally referred to as Refreshment Sunday, based on the Gospel's Feeding of the Five Thousand, and the color for the day was changed from the Lenten purple to rose. Strictly speaking, however, with the present use of the revised traditional One-Year Series of Scripture readings as well as of the new Three-Year Series in *Lutheran Worship* (1982), the former characteristics of these two Sundays have somewhat lost their significance.

10

Decorations in Sacred Space

Many *symbols* adorn the furniture and appointments of the chancel and nave. The most common symbol, of course, is the cross. Crosses are carved into the woodwork. Crosses are set into the stained glass windows. Crosses are applied or embroidered on the paraments and sacred linens. Crosses are even painted on the plaster of the walls or ceiling of the church. The most important cross, however, is the chancel cross, placed on the altar, suspended from the ceiling, or attached to the liturgical east wall. No other cross, nor any other symbol or decoration, for that matter, should detract from the prominence that the chancel cross has (with the altar) as the focal point of the church's interior.

In addition to the cross, there are many other symbols that may decorate the chancel and nave.[1] When choosing symbols (including crosses) to use in the chancel or nave, on their appointments, or on the paraments or vestments, three points need to be kept in mind: number, placement, and style. First, while it is fitting to mark the most sacred spaces and objects with an appropriate symbol, the multiplication of symbols should be avoided so that the impact and meaning of the symbols are not diluted. Second, symbols, particularly crosses, should not be placed just anywhere, especially if that placement contributes to a cheapening or irreverent treatment of the symbol. For example, a cross placed on the floor would be trodden underfoot and thus dishonored. The third point, concerning style, is the one that is probably violated most often today. Symbols should be chosen that will harmonize with their environment. For instance, vestments which have modern, schematic designs on them are not really compatible with a more traditional interior of an older building. Perhaps that is a good argument for reverting to the practice of the congregation rather than the pastor owning the vestments. Another example of stylistic incongruity is to have paraments with profuse and elaborate symbols in a chancel that is already saturated with decoration and symbolism. The symbols compete with one another and drown each other out. In this case, the best solution would be to apply on the paraments a singular symbol (such as a simple cross) or none at all, since the color itself is symbolic of the season.

The use of *flowers* is another type of decorating that is common in many churches. They serve no liturgical function but help to set the mood or tone of an event, as they do when used in the home. The basic symbolic value of flowers is joyfulness, and as such they are an expression of the goodness and beauty of creation. For these reasons the use of flowers in the church may be either appropriate or inappropriate, depending on the season of the church year.

When employing flowers as decoration, the first matter that must be kept in mind is the type of floral arrangement. Must we always use real flowers, or may artificial flowers be used? Are the flowers to be cut, or may we use potted plants? The rule of thumb is that real flowers are to be preferred. This rule conforms to the principle that objects used in the house of God should be genuine. However, the use of artificial plants and flowers today is widespread, and their use is motivated by convenience and cost rather than deception or dishonesty. If one wishes to be consistent with the genuineness principle, then one should demand, for example, that all fabrics and carpeting used not be synthetic nor contain synthetic materials, or that all woodwork be solid and not veneer.

In fact, in some places it may be illegal to use real as opposed to artificial plants. Some states, for instance, have laws against using real Christmas trees in public buildings. Rather than not have a Christmas tree at all, a congregation may choose to use an artificial one. The thing to remember here is that whatever artificial decoration is used, it should convey the beauty and dignity of the house of God. In recent years some silk plants, for example, have been produced to look so authentic that it is difficult to distinguish them from the real thing. What should not be done is to let them collect dust or to use them when tattered or faded. Ultimately, there is no theological reason against using artificial plants or flowers. As indicated above, however, when possible the real thing is to be preferred.

What about potted plants? There is debate over this matter also. Again, there is no theological reason against the use of potted plants. Some have suggested that cut flowers are more appropriate because of the symbolism of sacrifice. As noted earlier, however, the symbolism of flowers (and plants) is that of the joy in the beauty and goodness of God's creation. The problem with potted plants often is the container. Some holiday plants come wrapped with gaudy foil or colored bows; these should be removed. The other problem with potted plants is that the container may leak. Carpeting, tile, fabric, and woodwork can be stained by water running from the pot. A suitable tray or plate should be placed under the container. Care should be taken to choose one that does not look cheap or undignified. The best solution is to use a tray made from the same material as the pot.

A second matter to consider in the use of flowers and plants is their number and placement. The guiding principle for the number of plants or flower arrangements is that they must be tasteful and not detract from the focal point of the chancel, namely, the altar and chancel cross. Too much floral decoration creates a visual distraction and may even appear extravagant. The rule was stated well by Lang: "It is better to err on the side of simplicity than to overdecorate."[2]

The placement of flowers is also a concern. They should never obstruct the view of the altar cross or any other significant decoration or symbol. Flower stands (vases mounted on floor standards) offer a number of possibilities within the chancel and may be placed on the floor of the nave where it adjoins the chancel. If positioned in the chancel itself, there should be two flower stands to flank the altar. In the nave one may suffice, as long as a balance can be achieved with the liturgical furniture. Regardless of where they are placed, flower stands should not interfere with the movement of the pastor, his assistants, or, if local custom, communicants approaching the altar rail to receive the Sacrament. Floral arrangements in vases may also be used. They may be placed on the gradine (or gradine shelf, if the altar is freestanding) but never on the mensa of the altar. If placed on the gradine, the arrangements (there should be two) are set between the candles and the altar cross, not at the ends of the gradine. Vases should harmonize with the other chancel appointments. Finally, flowers should not be placed in or on top of the baptismal font, pulpit, or lectern.

Another matter to be kept in mind when using flowers and plants in the church is their size and color. An excessively large arrangement will create the kind of visual distraction warned against earlier. If placed on the gradine, the arrangements should not be higher than the candles and altar cross. Color is important also. While all flowers in an arrangement need not match the color of the paraments, the arrangement as a whole should harmonize with them and be consistent with the festival or season of the church year.

The final matter to be considered is this: What should be done with flowers or plants after they have been used for the service? A custom that is worthy to be continued is to send them to someone who is sick, hospitalized, or homebound. Another practice is to let the person who requested and paid for them take them home. In no circumstances should they be left in the chancel to wilt. Also, empty vases and floor standards should not be left in the chancel but put away in the sacristy.

Certain times of the church year make the use of plants and other decorations appropriate while other times do not. During the more restrained or somber seasons of Advent and Lent, for example, flowers would not be suitable.[3] On the other hand, seasonal decorations can add beauty to the church building and contribute to the festiveness of the celebratory feasts of Christmas and Easter.

The celebration of *Christmas* has become the preeminent holiday in American culture. Since the cultural holiday begins already on the day after Thanksgiving, care must be taken not to let the church's celebration of Christmas encroach on the season of Advent. Moreover, in addition to excluding pagan and secular symbols of the holiday, garish decorations such as flashing and colored lights are to be avoided. In the exuberance of members to celebrate the season, however, it may be difficult at times to curb some of the excesses.[4]

Fir trees and other greenery are the most common decorations for Christmas. Trees may be placed in the chancel and/or nave, and different types of greenery can adorn windows and columns. The trees need not be decorated, but if they are, the most suitable decorations are *chrismons*, white colored ornaments in the shape of Christian symbols (especially the symbols associated with the Christmas season). Electric lights are not recommended, but if it is local custom to use them, then the small, nonflashing white lights should be insisted on. As with other decorations, none of the greens should obscure or detract from the altar and chancel cross.

Candles are also popular accessories for Christmas decorating, especially because of the symbolism of light that is associated with the season. If the congregation has candelabra that are not used at all times, it would be most appropriate to bring them out for this festival. Candles placed on window sills and surrounded by simple greenery are attractive as well. Some congregations also have hurricane lamps on staves that attach to the aisle ends of the pews. All of these candles together, particularly for the Midnight Mass on Christmas Eve, create a very effective setting.

The flower for the Christmas season is the poinsettia, although several other kinds of flowers, for example, mums, could be used. Red poinsettias are the most popular color, but white is more in harmony with the celebration. An impressive display could be arranged using both colors. As with other flowers and greenery, their placement should be dignified and not interfere with the prominence of the altar and chancel cross. Because of the festivity of the season, Christmas flowers may be more numerous than during the nonfestival seasons. However, consideration of the fact that other decorations will probably be in use should be kept in mind so that the total effect is not overwhelming.

Another appropriate Christmas decoration is the Nativity scene. Local custom and/or the design of the chancel and nave may determine where this accessory is placed. Only Nativity scenes of high quality and craftsmanship should be used. This means that plastic figures should not be employed. Attention also needs to be paid to which figures are placed in the scene. Mary, Joseph, the Babe, and a few animals are always appropriate. Shepherds may be added for Christmas and the Sunday after. The Wise Men may replace them for the Epiphany.

Although not celebrated extensively in the secular sphere, *Easter* is the "queen of feasts" and the high point of the church year. The ornamentation of the chancel and nave should reflect that climax. Flowers are the primary decoration for Easter, although certain greenery, particularly the "victor palm branch," is also fitting. Unequaled in symbolism and beauty is the Easter lily. Other flowers may also be used, the preferred (or at least dominant) color being white. Placement of flowers and greenery should show concern for the altar and its cross. Because of the significance of Easter, the number of flowers may be more profuse than at any other time.

Since Easter lilies arrive from the florist in pots, some caution must be exercised. Potted plants may be positioned effectively around pulpit, lectern, and baptismal font. If there is room in front of the altar and they do not impede movement around the altar, plants may be placed there. If flowers are placed on the gradine, it may look better to cut five or seven blooms and arrange them in vases, rather than displaying potted plants with only two or three blooms. As at other times, the arrangements should not be higher than the arms of the cross. Garish appendages, such as ribbons and foil wrappers, should be removed from the potted plants.

Certain occasions may necessitate additional decorations being added to the chancel or nave. The *wedding service* is an occasion that may result in the most excess and require the greatest amount of tact and patience on the part of both the pastor and the altar guild. Many couples have a pre-conceived notion of what their "dream wedding" looks like and will want to do things in their own way. The best insurance against transgressing the standards and dignity fitting for the house of God is to produce a written policy on the decoration of the church for weddings and have the pastor pass it on to the couple as soon as it is confirmed that the wedding will take place at the church.

The most important thing to remember is that the wedding ceremony is set within a service in the house of God. The focus is on God, and the focal point of the service, as in other services, is on the altar and chancel cross. Anything that distracts from this principle must not be allowed. Since some couples engage professional florists, who may or may not be aware of this principle, it is always best that the florist contact the altar guild and do his or her work in cooperation with the altar guild or one of its members.

The rules that are in effect for other church services hold for the wedding service also. The use of flowers should be tasteful and not excessive. They should be arranged in consideration of the style and design of the chancel. Their colors should harmonize with the color of the time of the church year, since the paraments are those of the season and are not changed to accommodate decorative plans. Besides the chancel, flowers may also adorn the nave. The same considerations of taste and quantity should apply.

In addition to flowers other accessories may be desired to adorn or be used in the church. Some couples wish to have a floor runner down the center aisle. If the altar guild does not possess one, the couple may be able to rent one from the florist. For an evening wedding they may wish to use torches that attach to the ends of the pews. Sometimes bows are wanted for the aisle-ends of the pews; if used, they should not be gaudy.

If the chancel is not carpeted, a kneeling cushion should be provided for the place where the bride and groom kneel to receive the blessing. A popular addition to the service is the ceremony involving the so-called "unity candle." The theology and symbolism of this ceremony are ambiguous if not unbiblical. What unites the bride and groom are the pledges they exchange and the blessing of their marriage by God. In addition, their lives as individual persons do not cease with the lighting of the center candle and the snuffing of the two smaller candles. The "unity candle," therefore, should not be used.

Regardless of who does the decorating, it should be made clear whose responsibility it is to clean the chancel and nave. Decorations have to be taken down and certain items, if rented, need to be returned. These tasks may be delegated by the couple being married to their own friends and family. In any event, the church needs to be made ready for the next service. Once the church is returned to its prewedding service state, these preparations are the responsibility of the altar guild.

The other occasion that may require some additional arrangements, though perhaps not as many, is the *funeral service.* One appointment that is desirable is the funeral pall. Decorated with a cross or another sacred monogram, the pall is placed on the coffin in the narthex when it arrives in the funeral coach, and is removed in the narthex during the recessional. Besides equalizing the appearance of differing monetary values of caskets, it symbolizes the promise of resurrection given in Holy Baptism and directs the assembled mourners to this hope in Christ.

The only other decoration for funeral services are the flowers. As with other services, the amount of floral arrangements should not be overwhelming and their placement should not interfere with the prominence of the altar or chancel cross. Since the casket is placed at the head of the nave, the flowers should be placed on the nave level as well. Depending on the width of the nave, two or four arrangements should be enough. They should not, however, crowd out the paschal candle, baptismal font, or other liturgical appointments. Flowers should also not be placed on the coffin if a funeral pall is used. The only other caveat concerning floral arrangements is the following: "The ceremonies or tributes of social or other societies have no place within or after the service of the church."[5] This means that floral arrangements from lodges or other non-Christian organizations must not be displayed in the church.

Notes

1. See Paul H. D. Lang, *What an Altar Guild Should Know* (St. Louis: Concordia Publishing House, 1964), pp. 113–25, for illustrations and explanations of many of the different Christian symbols.

2. Lang, p. 108.

3. If the congregation observes Gaudete (the Third Sunday in Advent) or Laetare (the Fourth Sunday in Lent), flowers may be used on these Sundays.

4. See Carl Schalk, "Sketches of Lutheran Worship," in *A Handbook of Church Music,* ed. by Carl Halter and Carl Schalk (St. Louis: Concordia Publishing House, 1978), pp. 66–68. Schalk describes a rather extravagant Christmas celebration in Berlin in the church of Paul Gerhardt, confessional Lutheran preacher and hymn writer. Schalk comments that this service demonstrated "the extent to which a Lutheran congregation of the time could go in matters of liturgical freedom—possibly even exceeding the boundaries of 'good taste'—and still remain Lutheran in both spirit and substance."

5. Rubric 2 of the "Burial of the Dead," in *Lutheran Worship Agenda* (St. Louis: Concordia Publishing House, 1984), p. 169.

11

Paraments

The paraments are pieces of cloth that are hung on the main furniture of the chancel, namely, the altar, the pulpit, and the lectern. These cloth hangings are usually decorated with orphreys, symbols, and fringe. The material of the paraments should be of high quality. Traditionally silk damasks and brocades were used, although in recent years some synthetic fabrics have been employed as well. Whatever type of material is used, care should be taken so that the paraments do not become faded, dirty, or tattered. If symbols are applied, they also should be of fine quality. Embroidered silk and gold metallic appliques are available from ecclesiastical supply companies.

The color of the paraments follows the scheme of the liturgical colors (see chapter 6). Fabrics are available in several shades within each of the color groups and which shade is chosen will depend, to a certain extent, on the style and coloring of the chancel and its furniture. True colors are best. Wilder hues, such as neon reds or lime greens, should not be selected.

The parament which covers the front of the altar is called the *frontal*. It stretches from one end of the altar to the other (although not around the corners) and from the mensa to the floor (see fig. 11.1). Usually the frontal is attached to a piece of cloth the exact size of the mensa which covers the top of the mensa. This piece of cloth holds the frontal in place.

Over the frontal hangs a second parament called the *superfrontal*. Like the frontal the superfrontal extends from one end of the altar to the other but hangs down only about 8–12 inches from the mensa (see fig. 11.1). Also like the frontal, the superfrontal is attached to a second piece of cloth that lies on the mensa. Ordinarily the superfrontal is the same color as the frontal. If it is, it may be used alone in place of the frontal. Otherwise the frontal may be in a neutral color which coordinates with all of the superfrontals for the church year.

The foregoing description of the frontal and superfrontal follows the traditional usage of these two paraments for the altar. Variations will occur depending on the style of the altar and any decoration that it may have. For example, the front of the altar may bear a carved design, in which case only a superfrontal is used so that the design is not concealed. Or an altar may be square or oblong, and those dimensions will require modifications as well. An

Figure 11.1 Frontal, superfrontal , frontlets

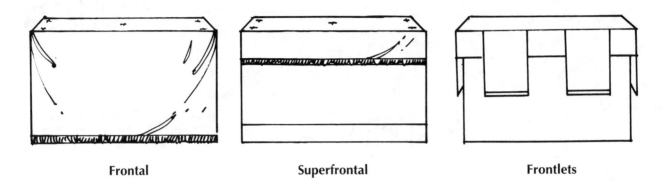

Frontal   **Superfrontal**   **Frontlets**

attractive alternative to traditional altar paraments is to use *frontlets*, two bands of material in the appropriate liturgical color (see fig. 11.1). Each band should be 6–8 inches wide and 12–18 inches long, attached to a second band of cloth that lies on the mensa, and suspended about 12–18 inches from the end of the altar.

Paraments of the same material as the frontal/superfrontal may also adorn the pulpit and lectern. These paraments have various names: *pulpit* and *lectern antependia* (singular *antependium*); *pulpit fall* and *lectern fall;* or *pulpit frontal* and *lectern frontal.* These hangings are usually square, although bands may be used as well (see fig. 11.2). Decoration may be similar to that of the frontal/superfrontal. Again, if the front of the pulpit or lectern is carved or decorated in some way, it may be best to eliminate these antependia or to design them so that they do not interfere with the other decoration.

The frontal, the superfrontal, and the pulpit and lectern antependia are the primary chancel paraments, but several others are included here because they are often made of the same kind of material and are of the same color as the primary paraments. One of these is the *chalice veil.* The chalice veil is square, usually from 18–24 inches on each side (see fig. 13.3). Its precise dimension is determined by the height of the chalice, since the edges of the veil should touch the corporal when the veil is draped over the chalice. An emblem or symbol may be sewn or embroidered on the center front of the veil.

The *burse* is an envelopelike case which is used to hold the corporal, Post-Communion veil, and purificators. It is made by sewing material over two squares of plastic or heavy cardboard, each about 8–10 inches square. Originally the burse was used to transport the sacred linens to and from the altar. If a credence is employed, the burse may still serve this function. In many congregations, however, where the sacred vessels and linens are set on the altar before the service and removed after, the burse may be unnecessary.

Many churches have returned to the use of the *funeral pall.* The funeral pall is 9–12 feet long and 6–8 feet wide, large enough to cover the casket and its carriage (see fig. 11.3). It may coordinate to the other paraments by being made of the same color and material or by having an orphrey of the same material. Today, however, most funeral palls are white since the pall symbolizes the righteousness Christians are clothed with in Holy Baptism. Adorned with a simple cross or symbol, the white pall may be used during any time of the church year. Traditionally the pall was made of silk damask or brocade, but today many high quality synthetics are employed as well. When used, the pall is placed over the casket in the narthex when the casket arrives at the church and is removed in the narthex after the service. Flowers should never be placed on the funeral pall.

As indicated at the beginning of this chapter, all of the paraments discussed here may be decorated with orphrey bands and symbols. In utilizing these decorations the principles of symbolism enunciated in chapter 10 should be observed. Also important in the selection of symbols is their appropriateness for the particular time of the church year. For example, a red pulpit antependium with a dove and seven flames would be appropriate for Pentecost but inappropriate for the festival of a martyr. A handbook on symbols with illustrations and explanations is helpful.[1]

Figure 11.2 Pulpit and lectern antependia, square and band

Figure 11.3 Funeral pall

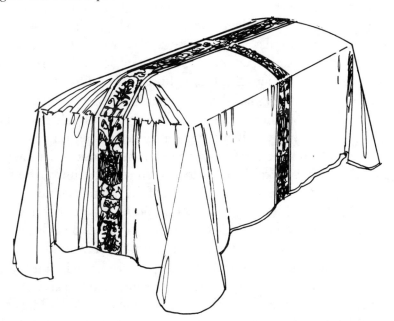

Notes

1. One such book is John Bradner, *Symbols of Church Seasons and Days* (Wilton, CN: Morehouse-Barlow, 1977).

12

Linens

The term *linens* refers to the cloths that cover the mensa of the altar as well as other cloth coverings used in the chancel. Ordinarily these cloths are made from real linen. Unlike the paraments, the linens are, in most cases, white in color and are not changed according to the color of the church year.

The linen placed directly on top of the mensa is the *cerecloth* or *cere linen* (see fig. 12.1). Originally this cloth was a heavy white fabric that had been treated with wax. Its purpose was to keep the dampness of the stone mensa from ruining the fair linen. On altars made of wood this protection is not necessary, although the cerecloth may still be used to protect the wooden mensa. In addition, this linen may serve as a cushion or padding to eliminate clanging when the sacramental vessels are placed on the altar. The cerecloth is the exact size of the mensa and should never hang over the edges.

A second linen may be placed over the cerecloth. It is called a *frontal linen* when it is attached to the frontal or superfrontal to hold either of those paraments in place, or simply a *protector linen* when it is not (see fig. 12.1). As the latter name implies, the purpose of this cloth is to protect the fair linen from the wax in the cerecloth. Like the cerecloth, this protector linen is the exact size of the mensa. It has no liturgical significance.

The third and chief cloth placed on the altar is the *fair linen* (see fig. 12.1). This cloth should be linen of the finest quality. Preferably it should be hemmed by hand and have embroidered on it five crosses, one in the center and the other four near the four corners of the mensa when the fair linen is laid on the altar. Unlike the cerecloth and protector linen, the fair linen hangs over the "north" and "south" ends of the altar. It should extend at least one-third of the way to the floor, preferably to within 6–9 inches from the floor. When the altar is not in use, a plain linen cloth may be placed over the fair linen and the altar to protect them from dust.

Similar to the fair linen is the *credence linen*. If a credence is employed, its linen should be of the same material as the fair linen on the altar. Its size, however, depends on the size of the credence table or shelf. The credence linen need not have any crosses embroidered on it or, if desired, one in the middle.

In some churches pictures, statues, and other objects are covered with cloths during the Lenten season as a sign of the solemnity of the season. These cloths are called *Lenten veils*. These veils are usually made of unbleached linen, although sheer fabric in either black or purple is also in use.

    Because the altar linens lie flat on the mensa they are subject to staining more than the paraments or other linens. The most common stains are from wine, candle wax, and soot from the candles or candle snuffers. Wine stains can be removed by sprinkling a little salt on the stain and then pouring boiling water through the fabric. Wax can be removed in one of two ways: place an ice cube on the wax, and then brush with a stiff brush or scrape with a knife; or place a paper towel or piece of cloth fabric beneath and on top of the wax and iron the wax into the towel or cloth. Soot is difficult to remove but try the following: Put a cloth under the stain; on a damp cloth put a few drops of dishwashing liquid (but not the kind for automatic dishwashers) and rub the stain lightly in a circular motion; rinse with warm water and repeat if necessary.

    Laundering the linens should be done with care. It used to be suggested that they be done by hand, but that is difficult with the larger pieces. There is nothing wrong with running these through the washing machine on the delicate cycle. They should be done separately, not with the other family laundry, and no starch or bleach should be used.

Figure 12.1 Fair linen, superfrontal, cerecloth, frontal

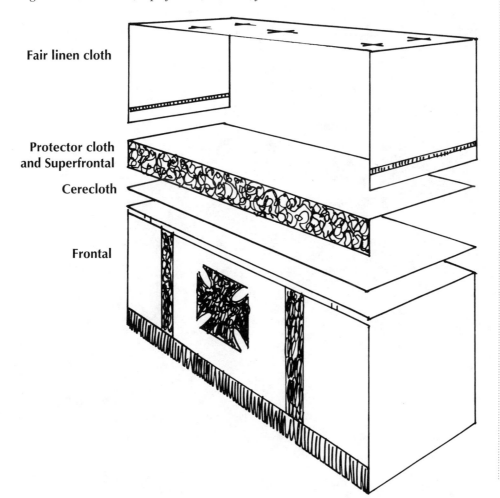

Fair linen cloth

Protector cloth and Superfrontal

Cerecloth

Frontal

13

For Holy Communion

The type of vessels used for Holy Communion will depend on the custom of the congregation. For example, a chalice or individual glasses or both may be used. The number of vessels will depend on the size of the assembly. The presiding minister may have one or more assistants distributing the blood of our Lord, in which case several chalices or trays of individual glasses may be employed. Regardless of the type and number of vessels, they should all be of the highest quality material. With the exception of glass cruets, individual glasses, and perhaps the lavabo, the sacramental vessels should be made of either silver or gold.[1]

There are several kinds of vessels that can be used for the sacramental bread. One of these is the *paten*. The paten is a round plate usually with the bowl or depression being slightly less in diameter than the chalice so that the paten fits into the mouth of the chalice (see fig. 13.1). The paten is the vessel on which the sacramental bread is consecrated and distributed. It should be large enough to hold a number of hosts sufficient to commune the entire assembly, thereby symbolizing what the apostle said: "Because there is one loaf, we, who are many, are one body, for we all partake of the one loaf" (1 Corinthians 10:17).

The *pyx* is a round or rectangular container with a cover to hold additional hosts (see fig. 13.1). Originally a sufficient number of hosts was transferred to the paten for the consecration, but today many ministers uncover the pyx and consecrate the hosts in it as well as on the paten. When the pyx is used to keep consecrated hosts against the next communion, then care should be taken not to mix unconsecrated hosts with the consecrated ones. If the pyx is used in this way, then a second pyx may be required to keep additional hosts for consecration.

A third kind of vessel for sacramental bread is the *ciborium*. The ciborium is shaped like a chalice but has a cover (see fig. 13.1). Originally the ciborium was used as a container for the consecrated hosts. After the service it was either placed on the altar and covered with a cloth or put into a cabinet called a *tabernacle*. The ciborium can be used in place of the paten (and pyx) to consecrate and distribute the body of the Lord. It can also be used with a paten, in which case it is then employed as a pyx to hold additional hosts.

Figure 13.1 Paten, pyx, ciborium

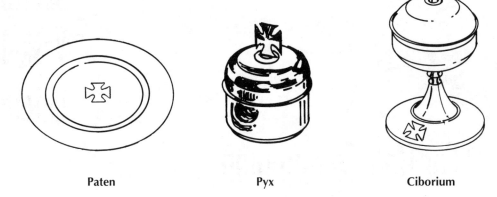

Paten   Pyx   Ciborium

A number of different vessels are used to hold and distribute the sacramental wine. First there is the *chalice*. A chalice is a cup that has three basic parts: the cup or bowl, the stem, and the foot (see fig. 13.2). Frequently in the middle of the stem (or on some modern designs in place of it) is a protrusion called a knop. Sometimes the chalice is also referred to as the *common cup*.

The *flagon* is a large vessel somewhat like a pitcher with a handle and a cover (see fig. 13.2). The flagon is used to hold additional wine. Wine is poured from the flagon into the chalice at the time of the consecration. Generally, however, the flagon is too large. In its place a glass or silver *cruet* or two may be used (see fig. 13.2).

In some congregations *individual glasses* are used instead of the chalice. These glasses fit into a template in a round tray (see fig. 13.2). Enough trays should be prepared to commune the entire assembly (the most common sized tray holds 40 glasses). Besides lacking the unifying symbolism of the one cup, individual glasses create much more work for the altar guild. In addition to the filling of the glasses there is the cleanup after the service. Each glass should be rinsed in a basin of water which is then poured into the ground or a piscina (or each glass filled with water which is then poured into a common receptacle to be emptied in the above fashion). Then the glasses need to be washed with soap and hot water and then rinsed and dried. Despite their popularity, plastic disposable glasses should never be used, for their use reflects the disposable attitude of our culture and as such contributes to a lack of reverence.

An additional vessel may also be employed at Holy Communion. The *lavabo* is a small glass or silver bowl used for the ceremonial cleaning of the presiding minister's hands. Water may be put into the lavabo ahead of time, or the assisting minister or acolyte, holding the lavabo in one hand under the presiding minister's hands, may pour water from the cruet over his hands into the bowl. The lavabo may also be placed on the end of the altar and water poured over the minister's hands in the above fashion. (In the latter case the lavabo should be placed on the altar at the time of the hand-washing and removed immediately afterward). This ceremony may take place during the offertory. It apparently symbolized the words of

Psalm 26:6: "I wash my hands in innocence, and go about your altar, O Lᴏʀᴅ." Restoring this usage may be beneficial in an age when many people are concerned about hygiene. It can be reassuring to some people to see the person who is going to handle the hosts cleaning his hands beforehand.

There are three sacramental linens that are used with Holy Communion. The first is the *corpora* (see fig. 13.3). The corporal is square, 18–21 inches on each side, depending on the depth of the mensa. It is made of the same quality of linen as the fair linen and has no embroidery except for a small cross in the center of the front edge 2–3 inches from the hem. The corporal is placed on the center of the altar. It is on this linen that the sacramental vessels are placed.[2]

The *purificator* is the napkin that is used to clean the chalice (see fig. 13.3). It is made of linen soft enough to be absorbent for this purpose. Usually the purificator is 11–13 inches square. It is folded into thirds and placed lengthwise ("north" to "south") over the chalice sitting on the corporal. If additional purificators are used (two or three are recommended), they are placed to the side of the vested chalice or on the credence. If there is a burse, they are put in it.

The last linen is the *chalice pall* (see fig. 13.3). The pall is a 7–9 inch square of glass, aluminum, or plastic covered tightly with fine linen. The exact size is determined by the diameter of the paten, over which the pall is placed. A simple cross may be embroidered on the center of the top of the pall, or a crown of thorns (with or without the cross; if with the cross, the crown of thorns surrounds it).

In some cases a *Post-Communion veil* will be used instead of a chalice veil. The Post-Communion veil is a white cloth that is draped over the sacred vessels on the corporal after the distribution of Holy Communion. It should be of the same fine material as that of the corporal.

If the presiding minister utilizes a lavabo, a small linen *towel* will be needed for him to dry his hands. An absorbent linen should be used and should be 9–12 inches square. After drying his hands, the minister folds it into thirds and drapes it over the lavabo, which is then removed to the credence or the sacristy.

The arrangement of the sacramental vessels and linens can be done in a number of ways, depending on the shape and location of the altar (see fig. 13.3). The basic setup is as follows: The corporal is placed in the center of the altar. In the middle of the corporal the chalice is set. Over the chalice the purificator, which is folded into thirds, is draped (lengthwise "north" to "south"). On top of the chalice and purificator the paten is set. If a celebrant's host is used, that host is placed on the paten and the other hosts are put

Figure 13.2 Chalice, flagon, cruet, individual glasses

Chalice

Flagon

Cruet

Individual glasses

into the pyx or ciborium. The paten is then covered with the pall, and over the pall the chalice veil is draped. Behind the chalice in the right corner is the flagon or cruet, and behind the chalice in the left corner is the pyx or ciborium. Additional purificators may be laid on the corporal to the right of the chalice. If a burse is used, the purificators are put into the burse and the burse is set on top of the chalice veil.

The above-described setup can be used with either a freestanding altar or an altar positioned against the "east" wall of the chancel. If the altar is freestanding, the setup perspective is from behind the altar, that is, where the presiding minister stands. If the altar is positioned against the wall, the perspective is, of course, from the front of the altar. With a square, freestanding altar, as noted above, the corporal will be placed in the center of the side of the altar where the presiding minister stands, close enough to the edge so that he can reach the sacramental vessels easily.

The foregoing description assumes that the chalice will be used for Holy Communion. If the congregation uses individual glasses there can be a problem, since the corporal is not large enough to accommodate the trays without appearing crowded. One solution is to set the tray (or stacked trays) to one side just partially on top of the corporal. Preferably a chalice will still be used (at least being offered to those who desire it). If the chalice is not used at all, the congregation may want to consider purchasing a ciborium, which can then be placed in the center of the corporal in place of the chalice. The ciborium, of course, will not be vested, although a white linen cloth may be placed over it as a veil. The practice of throwing a large, white veil over the stack of trays holding the individual glasses should be discouraged; it is not necessary. Finally, if the chalice is not used, there is no need for purificators.

The cleaning of the sacramental vessels and linens is also important. The linens can be laundered as described earlier in chapter 12. An additional stain that may be encountered is lipstick. Lipstick may be rubbed off onto the purificator when cleaning the chalice. The best way to remove lipstick is to use the procedure for removing soot stains. If the stain does not come out, then try the method for getting rid of wine stains. The silver and glass vessels can be washed by simply using hot soapy water and rinsing. They should be dried with a clean, absorbent towel so that they are not spotted. Occasionally the silver or gold may have to be polished. If that is necessary, then a good, high-grade polish without any abrasive agents should be used.

Notes

1. One reason for using silver or gold is that other metals can become discolored due to a chemical reaction with the alcohol in the wine. Another reason is that noble metals such as gold and silver are more hygienic (see Appendix D).

2. If the mensa is a large square, the corporal is placed in the center of the side on which the presiding minister stands.

Figure 13.3 Communion set up

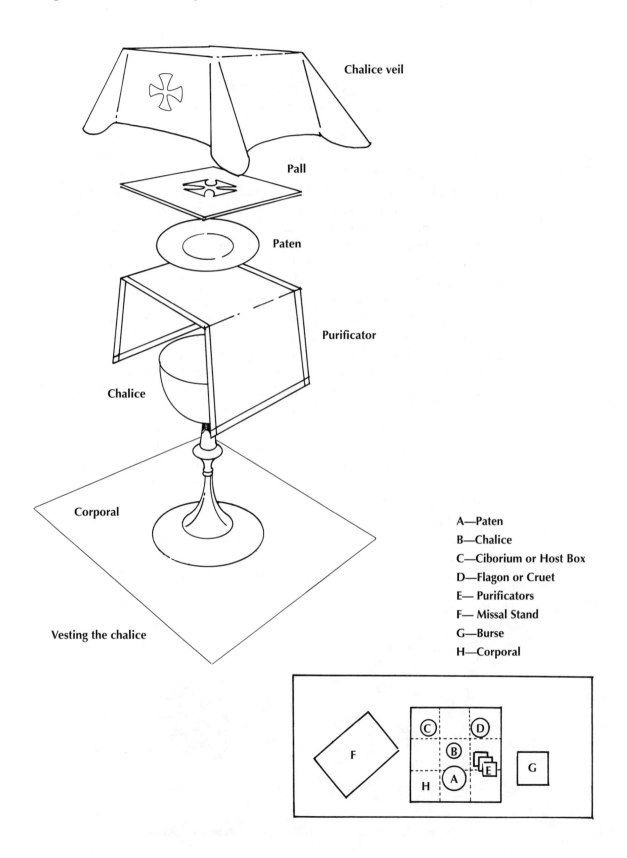

Chalice veil

Pall

Paten

Purificator

Chalice

Corporal

Vesting the chalice

A—Paten
B—Chalice
C—Ciborium or Host Box
D—Flagon or Cruet
E— Purificators
F— Missal Stand
G—Burse
H—Corporal

14

For Holy Baptism

Because the Sacrament of Holy Baptism is the rite through which a person enters the Christian community, it is properly done in the assembly of that community. The baptismal font should therefore be located in a position that underscores that significance. Many newer churches have placed the font in the narthex or in the center aisle of the nave. The location of the font at the front of the nave, however, ties it in to the altar and the pulpit. In either location the action of the rite should be clearly visible to the assembled congregation.

Most baptismal fonts are constructed of wood or stone. If the font is wooden, it will have a *baptismal bowl* to hold the water. This bowl is made of either metal (which should be silver or gold) or glass and usually can be removed to dispose of the water. A stone font ordinarily does not have a removable bowl. The water is removed through a drain hole in the bottom of the bowl. Some fonts are built so that there is a continuous flow of water, in which case adding and removing the water is unnecessary.

If water must be transported to the font a *ewer* or pitcher is used (see fig. 14.1). The water must be clean and may be slightly warmed. The ewer may also be used to remove the water from the font after the service.

In applying the water of Holy Baptism the minister may use his hand, applying as much as possible. Another way to apply the water is to use a *baptismal shell* (see fig. 14.1). This shell can be silver or it can be a real shell. If a real shell is used, it should be in perfect condition, not cracked or chipped.

After the water has been applied the minister uses a *napkin* to dry the

Figure 14.1 Ewer, baptismal shell

Ewer

Baptismal Shell

head or forehead of the baptized. This napkin should be of fine linen and may be embroidered with a cross. In some churches it is the custom to let the baptized keep this napkin. The minister may also use a *towel* to dry his hands after the application of water. This towel should also be of fine linen and may be embroidered with a cross (for both see fig. 14.2).

Additional vessels, linens, and other items may be used according to the customs of a congregation. The rubrics of *Lutheran Worship* allow for a *chrisom* (not to be confused with *chrism*; see below), a white baptismal garment, to be put on the baptized (see fig. 14.2). This garment symbolizes "that Christ has taken away and borne your sin and put upon you his perfect righteousness."

Lutheran Worship also allows for the baptized to be given a candle, which symbolizes the light of Christ who is the Light of the world. This candle is lighted from the paschal candle or altar candle and can be used at home on the anniversary of the Baptism.

Some churches may be following the tradition of using *chrism*, a consecrated and usually fragranced oil. The oil is applied after the Baptism by making the sign of the cross on the forehead of the baptized. Oil symbolizes the Holy Spirit, and the action symbolizes that the baptized has been sealed in salvation by the Spirit.

During most of the Baptism the minister will be holding the service book in his hands. This means that he cannot hold the other items used in the rite. If it is convenient, they may be placed on the credence. If there is no credence, a suitable tray may be used. When a tray is used, an assisting minister or acolyte will have to hold it.

After the service the water should be removed (if the font does not have continuously running water) and the vessels and linens cleaned. The water in the bowl, or in the ewer if it has been drained from the bowl, should be poured into the piscina or onto the ground. It should not be poured into a common drain. The towel (and napkin, if retained by the congregation) must be laundered. Reverence for their use will mean that, as with the Communion linens, they will not be washed with the family laundry. The baptismal bowl should also be cleaned. If it is silver, it may have to be polished from time to time.

Figure 14.2 Towels, napkin, chrisom

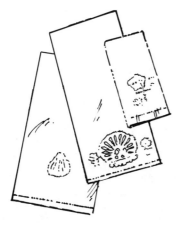

15

For the Clergy

In the Old Testament God commanded that certain types of garments be worn by the priests and other assisting ministers when they were performing liturgical duties. Although such garments were not commanded for the church, the church in Christian freedom has continued this usage. Vestments therefore continue to be worn by those performing liturgical duties in the Divine Service and other rites.

The purpose of vestments is twofold: liturgical and universal. The liturgical purpose of vestments is that they mark the person who is performing a specific liturgical function, such as the presiding minister, the assisting minister, the acolyte, the organist, and others. The universal purpose of vestments is that they provide continuity in the church. In different times and in different places the common vestments of the church have served as a mark of unity of the one holy catholic and apostolic church.

Because vestments were not commanded in the New Testament, the history of their development is long and varied.[1] The earliest vestments seem to be derived from official dress in the Roman Empire. These garments gradually changed in style until the Reformation period, when the radical reformers determined to rid the church of any mark that set the clergy off from the laity. In the 19th and 20th centuries, however, there has been renewed interest in the liturgical vestments of the church.[2] There is also a varied development in vestments among the different "rites" of the church. The Roman and other Western churches use vestments that are similar to one another, while the Eastern Orthodox churches follow another tradition of ecclesiastical vesture.

Vestments, then, by definition are special garments worn by persons in the performance of their liturgical duties. They can be simple or ornate. They can be worn by clergy and laypeople. Since the clergyman or ordained minister is the most common (and sometimes only) officiant in Lutheran churches, this chapter will be devoted to the vestments of the clergy.

The basic vestment is the *alb* (from the Latin *albus* meaning "white"). The alb is a full-length garment with long sleeves (see fig. 15.1). Originally it was made from white linen, but today it is most commonly made from cotton, polyester, or a cotton-polyester mix. The alb comes in three styles. The traditional alb is cut from the collar about 12 inches down the center so that it slips

Figure 15.1 Alb, cincture, and stole

Figure 15.2 Chasuble

over the head and is closed with buttons. The cassock alb overlaps in the front and is fastened in two or three places with snaps or velcro. Both of these styles are secured around the waist with a rope or band called the *cincture*. The contemporary alb either fits over the head or has a concealed zipper at the neck which allows over-the-head vesting. This type of alb does not require a cincture.

The alb is the usual eucharistic vestment. This means that it is the vestment that the minister ordinarily will wear for the celebration of the Lord's Supper. Along with the alb he will also wear a *stole* (from the Greek *stole* meaning "long, flowing robe"). The stole is a narrow band of cloth, usually of the same fabric as the paraments, which drapes over the neck and down the front of the alb (see fig. 15.1). It is about nine feet long. The traditional stole is about 2½ inches wide at the neck and widens to five inches at the ends. The broad stole has a uniform width of about five inches. In addition to being of the same fabric as the paraments, the stole is also the same color, that is, the color of the liturgical season.

Along with the alb and stole the minister may also wear a *chasuble* (from the Latin *casula*, which means "little house"). The chasuble is a poncholike garment that fits over the alb and stole. Its shape is either semicircular, elliptical, or rectangular (see fig. 15.2). Like the stole, the chasuble will also reflect the color of the liturgical season. This means that its primary color will be that of the liturgical season, or that the material will be of a neutral color with an orphrey or some other ornamentation coordinating with the color of the liturgical season. Since the chasuble is a eucharistic vestment, it is properly worn only at services in which the Lord's Supper is celebrated. Accordingly, it may be worn for the entire divine service, or it may be put on immediately before the commencement of the eucharistic liturgy (either during the offering or the offertory).

Because of the freedom of liturgical vesture, and the history of such garments, other types of vestments may also be worn by the minister. Common also in Lutheran churches is the use of the cassock and surplice. The *cassock* is similar to the alb. It is a long, close-fitting garment with long sleeves (see fig. 15.3). Traditionally, it was the "everyday attire" of the clergy, that is, the garment which they wore when they were not officiating in a service. Then it became the garment over which the clergyman wore his other vestments. The color of the cassock is black.

The *surplice* (from the Latin *super* meaning "over" and *pellicium* meaning "robe of fur") is a garment worn over the cassock (see fig. 15.3). Historically, it is a white garment that was a substitute for the alb. In areas where the climate was colder, the minister wore a garment of fur instead of an alb so that he could keep warm. Over this garment of fur the surplice, a white garment resembling an alb, was worn. Today the cassock and surplice is an alternative to the alb. Liturgically, the alb is worn for services in which Holy Communion is celebrated, while the cassock and surplice is worn for other services (that is, the Service of the Word, or Matins or Vespers). It might be of interest to note that the somewhat widespread adoption of the surplice-and-stole combination in Lutheran circles—for which there is no Lutheran precedent—represents an importation of 19th-century Anglican use.

Since vestments are an *adiaphoron* (that is, a matter that is neither right nor wrong), we must also mention the vestment called a *gown*, or, more precisely, a *Geneva gown*. This garment is a black gown that looks like a graduation robe. In fact, the origin of this garment is that it was a gown worn by professors and judges. It is usually worn with a white, ruffled collar, or two bands which are suspended from the neck called a *beffchen*. This type of garment, however, has no liturgical significance and was usually worn as a statement against the more "Roman" type of ecclesiastical dress. Nevertheless, it was common during the "protestantizing" period in the history of the Lutheran church.

When the minister must go outdoors, especially in areas where colder weather is common, he may wear a *cope*. The cope is a long, capelike vestment. It is open in the front and fastened in one place with a clasp (see fig. 15.4). It is used when the minister must go outside, as in a funeral procession. Liturgically, it has also become a vestment that is proper for noncommunion services, such as Matins or Vespers. Ordinarily it is of a neutral color with an orphrey that is proper to the liturgical season.

As indicated earlier, vestments are essentially an adiaphoron. They may be used according to custom and preference. The minister(s) will be sensitive to their proper usage and will try to be cognizant of their historical and ecclesiastical significance.

Finally, the altar guild should be mindful of the fact that, in addition to the liturgical significance of vestments, there is also their universal purpose. This means that the vestments which a minister wears are not properly his possession, but the property of the congregation. The implication of this fact is that most, if not all, of the vestments which are used in a congregational setting should be the property of the church. The altar guild of the local church will make sure that the presiding and other ministers of the church are properly attired for whatever functions they perform. Whatever vestments are needed for their minister(s), the altar guild (and congregation) should readily supply.

Notes

1. See, for example, *The New Westminster Dictionary of Liturgy and Worship*, ed. by J. G. Davies (Philadelphia: Westminster Press, 1986), s.v. "Vestments," by Gilbert Cope.

2. It should be noted that vestments were always in use in liturgical churches. It was only the more radical Protestant groups that discarded them. This "protestantizing" influence, however, was also felt in the Lutheran churches.

Figure 15.3 Cassock and surplice

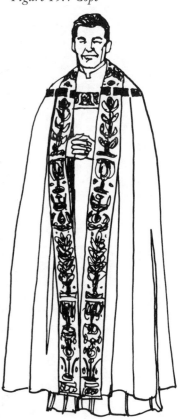

Figure 15.4 Cope

16

For the Lay Assistants

Along with the vestments of the minister or ordained clergyman, it has been customary in liturgical churches to provide vestments for those persons who assist in the conduct of the liturgy. Those persons include the assisting minister or lector, the servers (acolytes, crucifer, torchbearers, and thurifer), the organist, and the choir. Not all services will utilize all of these assistants. Common in many churches, however, are the assisting minister, the acolytes, and the organist.[1]

One type of garment for the assistants is the *cassock*. This is the same vestment that the presiding minister may wear. Cassocks in various colors are available from ecclesiastical supply houses for the servers and the choir, but these garments should be black. Over the cassock a *surplice* or *cotta* may be worn. The surplice is the same as that of the presiding minister. The cotta is like a surplice, except that it is shorter in length and has shorter sleeves (see fig. 16.1). Usually the cotta is worn by servers, the organist, and the choir. The assisting minister or lector should be vested with a surplice.

The other type of garment for the assistants is the *alb*. Again, this is the same garment that may be worn by the presiding minister (see fig. 16.2). Colored cinctures are available for servers and others, but as with the colored cassocks these should not be used. A plain, white cincture is preferred.

Which type of vestments should the assistants wear? The general rule of thumb is that, if the presiding minister wears a cassock and surplice, the assistants should wear cassocks and surplices (or cottas). If the presiding minister wears an alb, the assistants should wear albs. Sometimes the choir is exempted from this rule. Especially if the choir is large, purchasing and maintaining two sets of vestments may be unnecessarily expensive. Those who are "up front," however, assisting the presiding minister (assisting minister, lector, servers) should be attired in the same type of vestment that the presiding minister is wearing.

Various accessories for the vestments of lay assistants are available from the ecclesiastical supply companies. One of these accessories is the so-called choir *stole*, usually shorter and narrower than the stole that the ordained clergyman wears. The practice of nonordained persons wearing a stole should be avoided, however, since it is confusing. The so-called *v-neck stole*, which is really a type of collar, may be worn, but is unnecessary. There is also something called a *deacon's stole*, which is similar to the minister's stole but draped over only one shoulder. The other kind of accessory is the *pectoral cross*, a cross hanging on a chain from the neck and resting on the chest. Traditionally, the pectoral cross was worn only by the bishop as a mark of his office. Since the pastor of a local congregation is the "bishop" of that church, he may wear one. Historically, however, the bishop is an ecclesial supervisor in the larger church, so the practice of wearing a pectoral cross may better be reserved for him. Besides the issue of confusion, any of these accessories are really superfluous. The wearing of an alb or cassock/surplice/cotta is sufficient in designating the assistants for the special function or service that he or she may provide.

Another type of vestment that needs to be mentioned, since it is also sold by ecclesiastical supply houses, is the *gown*. Gowns are most commonly worn by members of the choir, although they are available for other assistants as well. These gowns resemble academic gowns worn in commencements and other academic functions, because that is what they really are. Gowns, therefore, should not be worn by any of the worship assistants since they are academic and not ecclesiastical in character.

Although they are not worship assistants, persons who are going to be baptized or confirmed are sometimes also vested. The baptismal garment is called a *chrisom* and usually looks like a small, white poncho. The confirmation garment should be similar as a reminder of the confirmand's Baptism. Instead of a poncholike garment, a white capelike garment may be appropriate.[2] Not recommended are the confirmation gowns that can be bought or rented. These gowns are mostly academic in design, and that is the connotation that they often give. These are therefore not suitable for confirmation, since the rite of confirmation is not a graduation from anything.

As indicated above, the assistants have been designated for a special function or service in the congregation. It is entirely appropriate, therefore, and preferable, that such assistants be properly attired. In some congregations it is the custom for lay assistants to wear ordinary dress, that is, clothes that they ordinarily wear to church. Although vestments are an adiaphoron, as stated in the previous chapter, the practice of assistants wearing ordinary dress should not be encouraged. As assistants, they have been chosen and (it is hoped) trained for their specific roles in helping the presiding minister conduct the service. Their vesture, therefore, is a mark of that calling.

The maintenance of vestments, like that of the paraments, is the responsibility of the altar guild, particularly the vestments that are the property of the congregation. Vestments that are manufactured from washable fabrics may be laundered by the altar guild, while vestments of delicate and nonwashable fabrics should be sent to a professional dry cleaner. Vestments should be laundered frequently to keep them free from odor and soiling. Those fabrics that need

Figure 16.1 Cassock and cotta

pressing should be pressed. Rips, tears, loose buttons, and so on should be repaired immediately. It is important to keep vestments looking neat and clean so that the minister and his assistants do not appear slovenly.

Storage of the vestments also requires the attention of the altar guild. Many of the garments can be hung on coat hangers, but the thin, wire hangers should be avoided since they leave impressions on the yoke of the garment. Some vestments may have to be folded and put in drawers, but care should be taken in order to eliminate any fold lines. It may be wise to have an iron and ironing board in the sacristy so that quick touch-up jobs can easily be done.

Figure 16.2 Server in traditional alb

Notes

1. The role of the assisting minister varies. According to the rubrics in *Lutheran Worship Altar Book* (St. Louis: Concordia Publishing House, 1982), p. 11, the assisting minister does the portions in the service marked **A** or **L.** In the Divine Service, these parts are the petitions of the Kyrie, the introduction to the Hymn of Praise, the Old Testament and Epistle readings, the petitions in the Prayer of the Church, the distribution of the Lord's blood, and the Post-Communion Collect. At a minimum, most assisting ministers read the two Scripture readings and assist with the distribution of the Sacrament. If, for instance, the person reads only the first two readings, he is customarily referred to as the lector.

2. See Paul H. D. Lang, *What an Altar Guild Should Know* (St. Louis: Concordia Publishing House, 1964), p. 48.

17

For the Seasons

Each season of the church year has its own special emphases and appointments that will be used. The altar guild should review these matters ahead of time so that appropriate items and supplies may be readied or obtained. Since each season or festival day begins on the eve of that season or festival (technically at sundown), the time for preparation is on the day before. The best time is usually during the afternoon before. Exceptions for particular festivals will be noted as they occur.

Advent

Focus

The season of Advent is a time for preparation for the coming of Christ, both his coming in the incarnation at Christmas and for his second coming at the end of the world as King and Judge. The readings of the lectionary reflect a reversal of this order, the earlier part of Advent devoted to Christ's second coming and the part of Advent nearer to Christmas to his first coming. The chief emphasis of Advent is on preparation. In earlier years that preparation, like Lent, was markedly penitential. Since the liturgical revisions of the 1960s, however, Advent preparation has become more anticipatory and hopeful in character. The services and appointments of the Advent season should reflect the spirit of anticipation.

Color

The traditional color for Advent is purple, marking Advent more as a penitential season. The optional color for Advent is blue. According to some, blue is the preferred color since it better reflects the spirit of anticipation and hope. If blue is used, the color should be light blue or royal blue; a blue that is too dark would look too much like purple and the reason for using blue, as opposed to purple, would be nullified.

Customs

Common in Lutheran churches today is the use of an Advent wreath, a wreath of evergreen branches with four candles at equal distances from one another. The Advent wreath is used to mark the four weeks of Advent, with one candle being lighted for each week of Advent (that is, one lighted for the first week, two lighted for the second week, and so on). This use of the Advent wreath symbolizes "the age before the coming of Christ, when the light of prophecy concerning the Messiah became brighter and brighter till He Himself came and said, 'I am the light of the world.' "[1]

Formerly it was said that the color of the candles should be white. But colored candles may also be used. If the paraments of the church are purple, the wreath candles should be purple. If the paraments are blue, the candles should be blue. (One candle may also be rose or pink, lighted on the Third Sunday in Advent; see page 46.) Because the Advent wreath is an appointment for the preparatory season, it should be used only during Advent. This means that the practice of including a "Christ candle," which would be lighted on Christmas Eve (after the *end* of the Advent season), should be discontinued. Of course, this may necessitate some creative arrangement of the greens, since much of the hardware offered by ecclesiastical arts companies includes a receptacle for such a candle.

Generally, the decorating of the church during Advent should not be too elaborate. Advent is a season of preparation for something greater. While not as austere as the Lenten season, the mood of Advent does call for some restraint in deference to the "tidings of great joy" that will be proclaimed at the nativity and during its season. Candles should be used at a minimum.[2] Seasonal greenery may be placed in the church, but it should remain undecorated so as not to appear too festive. Banners may also be hung but should be kept simple in color and style in keeping with the mood of the season.

A problem that has become more prevalent is keeping the congregation from wanting to put out its Christmas decorations too early. The cultural celebration of the Christmas season between Thanksgiving and Christmas has had its influence on our church life as well. Usually, the point of contention in a congregation is that, with the increasing number of preparations and obligations that people have as Christmas approaches, they need to be able to put the congregational Christmas tree up early. Ideally, if a congregation puts up a tree, it should not be put up until after the Fourth Sunday in Advent. When December 24 falls on a Sunday or Monday, it may be difficult to prevail. If it is absolutely necessary to put up a tree earlier, then it may be put up during the week before the Fourth Sunday in Advent. However, if the tree is decorated with lights, the lights should not be turned on until after the Fourth Sunday in Advent. In any event, the altar guild will strive to keep the style and decoration of the church with the spirit of Advent. Careful planning and budgeting of time will help the altar guild make the transition from Advent to Christmas.

Christmas

Focus

Christmas is the season in which we hear the "tidings of great joy" that the Savior of the world was born in Bethlehem. The Second Person of the Trinity had to become man in order to redeem man. After the Feast of the Resurrection, then, the Feast of the Nativity is the greatest in the church. The atmosphere and appearance of the church, in addition to its message and music, reflect the exceeding gladness of this celebration.

Color

The color for Christmas and its season is white. White symbolizes divinity, eternity, purity, light, and joy, so this color is most appropriate for celebrating the incarnation of the God who came to redeem mankind. Because white is also the color for Easter and its season, the altar guild will take care that the white paraments of Christmas display only Christmas symbols.

Customs

Because of the association of light and joy with Christmas, one of the most appropriate and effective decorations of the church is the candle. If the congregation has candelabra that were removed for Advent, the celebration of Christmas would be the appropriate time to bring them back into use. Other candles, such as candles on the window sills or in candle stands that stand in the center aisle of the nave, would also be fitting. The multiplication of candles (so many so that the electrical lights in the church are not needed) provides a very effective setting for the Midnight Mass on Christmas Eve.

Flowers and greenery also help to beautify the church and aid in expressing the joy of the season. The flower most commonly used for Christmas decoration is the poinsettia. Greenery such as fir boughs or holly branches may be used to decorate windows, columns, and other architectural pieces (but not the altar, pulpit, or font).

As indicated above, it is common in Lutheran churches today to see a Christmas tree. If the tree is appropriately decorated and properly located, there is no reason for not continuing its use. Legend has it that the evergreen tree was first used for Christmas decoration by Martin Luther, although the custom seems to go back to Boniface, an eighth century missionary to the Germans. Tradition has it that the popularization of a Christmas tree used as a decoration in the church goes back to H. C. Schwan (1819–1905), the fourth president of The Lutheran Church—Missouri Synod, while Schwan was a parish pastor in Cleveland.

Evergreen trees may adorn the chancel or nave undecorated. If ornaments are desired, the best kind are *chrismons*, white wood or Styrofoam decorations cut in the shapes of Christian symbols, particularly those symbols associated with Christmas. If the glass, ball-type decorations are used, it is best to use just one or two colors, such as all red, red and green, all gold, red and gold, or all white. Many different colors should not be used, because it gives a gaudy appearance not appropriate for the church; nor, obviously, should secular or commercial figures be used. If trees are placed in the chancel, they may flank the altar sitting in either the sanctuary or the choir, depending on how the chancel is constructed. The tree or trees may also be located at the head of the nave. In either location, their size and decoration should not distract from the altar as the focal point of the worship space. Finally, it has become the practice in many congregations to use electric lights. It is better liturgical practice not to use such lights, but if they are used they should be the small white, nonblinking kind.

Another appropriate Christmas decoration is the Christmas crib or *crèche*. At a minimum, the scene would include Joseph, the Virgin Mary, the Infant, and perhaps a few animals. Shepherds and sheep may be placed around the grouping for Christmas, the Wise Men and their entourage replacing them for the Epiphany. The placement of this scene will depend on the size and arrangement of the chancel. If there is room it may be placed in the nave just below the chancel. Actually, anywhere is appropriate, as long as it is not in front of the altar. Also, the figures should be made out of ceramic, stone, or wood; plastic figures are cheap and unbefitting.

The shortness of the Christmas season (12 days) and the many arrangements that may have to be made mean that the altar guild will have a lot of work during this season. Careful planning and preparation will have do be done ahead of time. More altar guild members than usual may be involved in the guild's work. Provisions may have to be made for obtaining greenery or picking up floral orders. The placement of decorations and extra candles may be assigned. Although they are assigned extra duties and probably rushed for time, the members of the altar guild should not let these burdens distract them from the joy and festivity of the season.

Epiphany

Focus

Originally the Feast of the Epiphany of Our Lord overshadowed that of his nativity (as it still does in the Eastern churches), but through the development of liturgical traditions Christmas became the more important of the two festivals in the Western churches. Today the Epiphany emphasis in the West is on the manifestation of the Incarnate Lord to the world. This emphasis begins with the Feast of the Epiphany, January 6, which commemorates the visit of the Gentile Wise Men to the Babe of Bethlehem. This festival is one of great rejoicing and gladness, since the light of the world is revealed to the nations, "a light to lighten the Gentiles" (Nunc Dimittis).

The manifestation theme continues on the First Sunday after the

Epiphany, which celebrates the Baptism of Our Lord, when the voice from heaven revealed him as "my Son, whom I love; with him I am well pleased" (Matthew 3:17). The Sundays after the Epiphany continue to illustrate the manifestation of God in Christ Jesus. The traditional Gospel for the Second Sunday after the Epiphany, for example, is the wedding at Cana, where Jesus did the first of his signs and "revealed his glory" (John 2:11). The Epiphany season culminates in the Festival of the Transfiguration of Our Lord, when Jesus revealed his divine glory to the inner circle of his disciples. For the church today the Word of the Epiphany season continues to bring joy and awe to the faithful.

Color

Like Christmas, the color of the Epiphany and its season is white, the color of divinity, purity, and joy. On the Eve of the Second Sunday after the Epiphany, the paraments may be changed to green, since these Sundays, until the Eve of the Transfiguration, are considered by the dominant liturgical tradition to be "ordinary time." For the Festival of the Transfiguration the paraments are again changed to white. If the congregation wishes to continue to accentuate the manifestation emphasis, however, the color of the paraments for all of the Sundays after the Epiphany may remain white.[3]

Customs

Ordinarily there are no special decorations or customs for the Epiphany season as there are for the Christmas season. The Christmas greenery and decorations may be left up for the service on the Feast of the Epiphany but should be removed before the Baptism of Our Lord. The so-called "Moravian star," recalling the star which led the Wise Men to the Infant in Bethlehem, may be used as an appropriate additional appointment for the Epiphany service. On the First Sunday after the Epiphany, the Baptism of Our Lord, the church's baptismal font may be filled with water for the faithful to dip their finger in and cross themselves as a reminder of their own Baptisms. The Baptism of Our Lord was the first of his deeds to "fulfill all righteousness" and sanctify the waters of our Baptism. The usage of the full set of candles (eucharistic lights and floor candelabra) may continue throughout the Epiphany season as a reminder of the revelation of Christ "the Light of the world."

Lent

Focus

Lent is a time of preparation for Easter. In the early church it was a period of preparation for the Sacrament of Holy Baptism, which would take place on the Vigil of Easter. This preparation included fasting and other spiritual disciplines. Along with the emphasis on baptismal preparation, but perhaps not associated directly with it, was the use of Lent as the final period of penance in preparation for the rite of reconciliation on Maundy Thursday. After both of these purposes fell away, Lent became a period of general devotional preparation for Easter.[4] Nevertheless, the earlier emphases remained, and Lent was marked by rigorous penitence and austere spiritual discipline. During the period of Lutheran Pietism these strict practices were aided by an excessive fixation on the Passion of Jesus.

The modern observance of Lent, however, balances the penitential theme with the baptismal theme. Lent begins on Ash Wednesday with a call to repentance: "Return to the LORD your God, for he is gracious and compassionate, slow to anger and abounding in love" (Joel 2:13). But on the Sundays in Lent which follow, the emphasis is more on reflection on Baptism and renewal in faith and life. As James Brauer writes in his discussion of the church year, Lent "is a time for the discipline of learning and growing in faith, for repentance and for prayer, even for fasting to practice self-control and to heighten one's awareness of Christ."[5] For the altar guild, all of this means that the appearance of the chancel and nave will be the most restrained of the church year, so that with their full energy and devotion the worshipers may say, "Oh, come, let us fix our eyes on Jesus, the author and perfecter of our faith" (Gradual for Lent).

Color

The color for Lent is purple, symbolizing sorrow and repentance. For Ash Wednesday the alternate color is black, the color of mourning, humiliation, and death. Whatever color paraments are used for Ash Wednesday, they are changed to purple for Thursday and not back to the white of the previous Sunday (the Transfiguration).

Customs

Because the mood of Lent is subdued, ornamentation in addition to the paraments and standard appointments is inappropriate. One custom allows for pictures and statues, if they are not removable, to be covered with an unbleached linen or purple veil. The use of flowers may be discontinued during the season. In fact, as an expression of joy and beauty, flowers are really not suitable for Lent. Flowers should not be used on Ash Wednesday.

A medieval custom that has once again become popular is the imposition of ashes on Ash Wednesday, the custom from which the day derives its name. If this rite is to be used, ashes will need to be prepared. Traditionally, the ashes were made by burning the processional palms from the previous year's Palm Sunday and mixing them with a little oil. They are applied by the minister making the sign of the cross on the worshiper's forehead while speaking a Bible verse as a reminder of human mortality. A small basin of water and a towel will be needed for the minister to clean his hands after the imposition. This rite can be an effective spiritual symbol of the need for repentance: "For dust you are and to dust you will return" (Genesis 3:19).

Holy Week

Focus

Holy Week is the most dramatic and significant week of the church year. It begins with Jesus entering Jerusalem in a triumphal procession. As the days progress, however, triumph turns into tragedy. The crowds still listen to Jesus, but the religious leaders set in motion their plot to kill him. Jesus and his disciples withdraw to celebrate his last Passover, which is at the same time the inauguration of the new covenant meal of the Lord's Supper. Then come betrayal and abandonment. The climax of Holy Week is the death of our Savior on Golgotha and his burial in the garden tomb. From a human standpoint that should be the end of the story—a tragic story ending in deepest woe. However, it is not. The third day is yet to come.

Color

The color for Holy Week begins with scarlet, the color of royalty and passion. It is particularly appropriate for Palm Sunday, also called the Sunday of the Passion, a day of both joy and sorrow on which we sing: "Ride on, ride on in majesty! In lowly pomp ride on to die" (*Lutheran Worship* 105). The alternate color for Palm Sunday is purple, the color of Lent, also the color of royalty, and the color of repentance and sorrow. Either scarlet or purple may be used through Maundy Thursday.

With the celebration of Holy Communion on Maundy Thursday, the preferred color is white. If the Sacrament is not celebrated (contrary to Lutheran custom), then scarlet or purple is used. If the altar is not stripped after the Maundy Thursday service (see below), the paraments are changed to black for Good Friday.

Customs

There are a number of different liturgical customs for Holy Week, and, since the days come in quick succession, the altar guild will want to plan and be prepared ahead of time. One Holy Week custom is to have a procession with palms on Palm Sunday.[6] If the procession is done, palm branches will have to be ordered ahead of time. This order can be placed through an ecclesiastical supply company. If the imposition of ashes is done in the congregation, the altar guild will want to make sure to collect enough of the palm branches after the service in order to have sufficient ashes for the following year.

The rule during Lent is that flowers are preferably omitted. This is especially true for Holy Week, with two exceptions. Flowers may be used on Palm Sunday and Maundy Thursday. If used, they should be in harmony with the color of the day. On Palm Sunday palms would also be an appropriate ornamentation.

On Maundy Thursday the preferred service is the Divine Service. After the distribution, the service should quickly come to its end (for example, using only the Post-Communion Collect and the Benediction). Immediately after the Benediction, the minister(s), the altar guild, and servers may strip the altar.[7] This rite is symbolic of Christ's humiliation at the hands of the Roman soldiers. The altar's stripping should be done in an orderly manner. The candles need to be extinguished, and then the following are removed and carried to the sacristy: first the sacred vessels and linens, then the candles and missal stand (with book), and then the remaining linens and paraments. If there is an altar cross or crucifix on the gradine, it may be removed last. Following the stripping, the chancel gate (if there is one) is shut. It remains closed and the altar bare until the Vigil of Easter.

In the *Lutheran Worship Agenda* two services are provided for Good Friday: "Good Friday I" without Holy Communion and "Good Friday II" with Holy Communion.[8] According to the *Agenda*, "the older and more primitive custom is that Holy Communion not be celebrated on Good Friday."[9] There may be some circumstances, however, for celebrating Holy Communion on Good Friday. If the service includes Holy Communion, the vesting of the altar should remain simple. If altar paraments are used, they should be black. If the Good Friday service does not include Holy Communion, the altar should remain bare as it was after the stripping on Maundy Thursday. Regardless of which service is used, the pulpit and lectern may be vested. If they are, the antependia should be black.

A custom that may be used on Good Friday is the procession with a roughhewn cross.[10] A roughhewn cross is made of untreated tree limbs about 4–5 inches in diameter, the vertical extension being about 5–6 feet and the horizontal extension 3–4 feet, large enough to be seen but not so large that it is too heavy to carry. The cross is carried in during the service and is either placed in a stand before the altar or is leant against the altar or altar rail. Two tall candles may flank the cross.

Another type of service that is commonly done on Good Friday is the *Tenebrae*. Tenebrae is the Latin word for "darkness." During this service candles are extinguished after a number of Scripture readings, one candle after each reading. The altar guild will want to see to it that there are a sufficient number of candles for the readings. A candelabrum may be used (if the congregation has one), but this will limit the number of readings to the number of branches the candelabrum has.

Easter

Focus

Easter is the high point of the church year. On this day the Lord rose from the dead. Having conquered sin and Satan, he guarantees victory for us over death and the grave. Referring to the festival itself, Easter is the "queen of feasts." No preparation is too elaborate, and no observance is too jubilant. Referring to the season, Easter is the most celebratory time of the church year. The church observes this season over 50 days with three great feasts: the Feast of the Resurrection, the Feast of the Ascension, and the Feast of Pentecost.

Color

The color for Easter is white, symbolizing perfection, celebration, and joy. The alternate color for Easter is gold, the color of riches and glory. If gold paraments are available, they should be used only on Easter Sunday. The color white continues throughout the Easter season, including the Feast of the Ascension, until the Eve of Pentecost, when the paraments are changed to red. The red paraments should preferably not be the same that are used on festivals of martyrs, since the symbolism will be different. If the congregation cannot afford two sets of red paraments, then perhaps one of the paraments, such as the pulpit antependium, could come as two, one for Pentecost and one for the other festivals.

Customs

The Easter celebration may commence with the Vigil of Easter.[11] The Vigil begins with the Service of Light. A fire may be built outside for the opening of the liturgy. The paschal candle is lighted from this fire, or may be lighted in some other convenient way. The paschal candle is carried in procession into the church, and if individual candles were distributed, these may be lighted from the paschal candle. At the front of the nave the paschal candle is placed in its stand near the central approach to the altar. If the baptismal font is moveable, it would be appropriate to place the font in the center also. At the end of this rite, the individual candles may be extinguished. Then follows the Service of Readings. A few lights may be turned on. Then comes the Service of Holy Baptism. If there are candidates for Baptism, the usual preparations will be made. If there are no candidates, the font may still be filled with water for worshipers to dip their fingers into and cross themselves. Finally, there is the Service of Holy Communion. The altar candles are lighted and the rest of the lights turned on. The preparations for the Vigil are many, but the service is effective and worthwhile.

Traditionally the Easter Vigil was celebrated on Easter Eve, the evening before Easter. It may also be celebrated early Easter morning, before dawn or at least beginning before dawn. In either case, the service should remain simple. The more festive celebration of the resurrection should be reserved for the chief service on Easter Day.

Easter Day is the main service not only of the day but of the entire church year. Altar guild preparations, in addition to liturgy and music, should reflect that significance. The white paraments for Easter should be the best set that the congregation owns. The linens should be the finest. If the congregation has a special set of communion ware, it should be used.

The paschal candle, employed already in the Vigil, remains in use during the rest of the Easter season. If the congregation does not have a paschal candle, this is surely one appointment that can be considered necessary after the basic paraments and appointments. The paschal candle is lighted for each service for the rest of the Easter season. It is extinguished either on Ascension or Pentecost and then moved (see below). The symbolism of the paschal candle, reminding us of Christ's victory over the darkness of sin and death, is most appropriate for the Easter season. This symbolism will be appreciated also for services of the burial of the dead (see below), regardless of what time in the church year they occur.

Flowers may be used on Easter in quantities greater than on any other festival of the church year. The most common flower used is the Easter lily, but other flowers that are signs of new life and growth after the dead of winter, such as tulips and daffodils, may also be used. Nevertheless, the predominant color of all the floral decorations together should be white, the color of Easter. Flowers should not be placed on the altar itself, but may be placed at the foot of the altar. Whatever type or arrangement of flowers is used, they should not distract from the altar and crucifix but lead up to them to call attention to these focal points of the worship space.

Parades are always part of a great celebration. In the church such parades are called *processions*. Easter is suitable time to make use of them. The liturgical processions are primarily the entrance procession and the Gospel procession. For the entrance procession the following may be needed: processional cross/crucifix, torches (two), thurible, an altar book or lectionary, and festive banners. For the Gospel procession (when the minister reads the Gospel from the middle of the nave) any of the preceding may be used, but at a minimum a lectionary or Gospel book is needed. This book should be large and elegant enough to reflect the honor that we accord the Word of God. Traditionally, the book carried in procession was also accompanied by torches and thurible.

The Sundays after Easter continue the celebratory themes, rites, and decorations indicated above. It is proper to do so, but they should not be quite so elaborate that they overshadow the prominence of Easter Day. If the rite of confirmation is not conducted on Palm Sunday, as is the custom in many Lutheran congregations, it is prevalent to do so during the Easter season. This season is quite appropriate for confirmation with its emphasis on baptismal celebration and the renewal of life. If confirmation is conducted at this time, the altar guild may be involved in the extra preparations.

The Ascension of Our Lord always falls on a weekday (Thursday), and it is becoming more common in Lutheran churches to hold services on this day, since it is one of the major festivals of the church year. The predominance of white continues, reflected both by the paraments and other decorations. No particular liturgical preparations need to be made. Traditionally, the paschal candle is extinguished at this service. Afterward it is moved to a place near the baptismal font and is used thereafter for Baptisms and funerals.

The conclusion of the Easter season comes with the season's third great festival, the Feast of Pentecost. On this day the risen Lord sent his Holy Spirit to the chosen Twelve and the one holy catholic and apostolic church came into being. The color of the day is red, and other ornamentation (flowers and banners, for example) may reflect this. The more modern custom with the paschal candle is to extinguish and move it on this day. After Palm Sunday, Pentecost is perhaps the most common day for conducting the rite of confirmation. As the third great festival of the church year (after Easter and Christmas), preparation and observance indicate the joyous mood of this feast.

Time after Pentecost

Focus

This period of time is the third division of the church year and comprises about one half of the calendar year. The time begins with the Feast of the Holy Trinity, a celebration of the mystery of God, three in person but united in substance. This feast is the First Sunday after Pentecost. The following Sundays (sometimes referred to as Sundays after Trinity Sunday) focus on the teaching of the Lord and its application to the lives of Christians. The season concludes with the Sunday of the Fulfillment, pointing to the second coming of Christ and the fulfillment of time. An option is to observe Christ the King Sunday as the last Sunday of the church year, pointing to his second coming when all things come under the reign of the one King.

Color

The color for the Holy Trinity is white, since that is the color of divinity and perfection. On the remainder of the Sundays after Pentecost, including the Sunday of the Fulfillment, the green paraments are used. Should Christ the King Sunday be celebrated, the paraments are again white. Because the time after Pentecost is such a long time, the altar guild may want to have two sets of green paraments. A set of lighter (but not lime) green could be used for the first part of the season, signifying new life and growth. A set of paraments in a deeper green could be used for the latter part, symbolizing the deeper teaching of the Lord in the later Sundays after Pentecost and the growth toward maturity that it requires.

Customs

There are usually no special customs or preparations that require the attention of the altar guild for the Sundays after Pentecost. The liturgy and ceremony will be simpler, indicating that this season is now "ordinary time." Flowers, banners, and other decorations may be used but should not be as elaborate as for the more festal times of the church year.

Other Festivals and Occasions

During the Time of Christmas and the Time of Easter the Sundays and major festivals of these times have precedence over the minor festivals and occasions (see chapter 5). Minor festivals and occasions, of course, may be celebrated during the week if they fall on a weekday. If they fall on a Sunday, they may be observed on the following day, Monday.

During the Time of the Church there is more latitude. Except for the Feast of the Holy Trinity, a major festival, a lesser festival may be observed on a Sunday of "ordinary time" or "green Sunday" (so called from the color of the paraments). The following are perhaps the most commonly celebrated festivals and occasions of ordinary time:

The Festival of St. Michael and All Angels falls on September 29 but may be observed on the Sunday following. This festival commemorates the role of angels, particularly St. Michael the Archangel, in God's plan of salvation and their service to God and mankind. The color for the day is white, which symbolizes eternity and perfection.

Reformation Day falls on October 31 but may be observed on the preceding Sunday. On this day we recall the work of God in preserving and reforming the church in times of trial and for giving the church teachers and defenders of the truth. The color for Reformation is red, the color of zeal and martyrdom.

All Saints' Day occurs on November 1 but may be observed on the following Sunday. The day commemorates not only all the martyrs but all the people of God, living and dead, who form the mystical body of Christ. The color is white, pointing to eternity and perfection which the saints now enjoy.

It has become almost universal in America for Christian churches of all confessions to observe the National Day of Thanksgiving, the fourth Thursday in November. On this occasion the church thanks God for creating and preserving us and giving us all that we need for body and soul. The color of the day is white.

Other festivals and occasions may be observed as the congregation decides. These and the above named four observances require no special preparations by the altar guild. If there is some local custom or usage to be included in these services, the altar guild will stand ready to assist.

Notes

1. Paul H. D. Lang, *What an Altar Guild Should Know* (St. Louis: Concordia Publishing House, 1964), p. 99.

2. If the congregation has floor candelabra that are used in addition to the eucharistic lights on the altar or gradine, it would be fitting to remove the candelabra from the chancel during Advent.

3. This is supported by Carl F. Weidmann in *A Manual for Altar Guilds*, third ed. (New York: Ernst Kaufmann, 1949), p. 52; Luther D. Reed in *The Lutheran Liturgy*, rev. ed. (Philadelphia: Fortress Press, 1960), pp. 480–84; and Lang,

p. 106. These works were all written before the revision of the lectionary in the 1960s. Since the "gesima" Sundays were dropped and the Epiphany season extended, the practice of using white throughout the Epiphany season could in principle also be extended.

4. On the history of Lent, see *The New Westminster Dictionary of Liturgy and Worship*, ed. by J. G. Davies (Philadelphia: Westminster Press, 1986), s.v. "Lent," by R. F. Buxton.

5. See James Brauer, "The Church Year," in *Lutheran Worship: History and Practice*, edited by Fred L. Precht (St. Louis: Concordia Publishing House, 1993), p. 166.

6. See *Lutheran Worship Agenda* (St. Louis: Concordia Publishing House, 1984), p. 35.

7. See the *Agenda*, p. 39.

8. In the *Agenda*, p. 48 and p. 58 respectively.

9. *Agenda*, p. 57.

10. In the service "Good Friday I" (*Agenda*, p. 51) or a similar service.

11. See the liturgy and notes in *Lutheran Worship Agenda*, pp. 73–90.

18

For the Services

Each service of the church has its own needs and appointments. The altar guild will need to plan ahead so that the appropriate items and supplies are at hand. Since the conduct of these services will be affected by the work of the guild, guild members must be dependable in carrying out their assignments. In addition, they must have an attitude of reverence, both while working in the house of God and toward the objects which are set aside for holy use.

The Divine Service

This manual assumes that the chief service of the week is the Divine Service, the service of Word and Sacrament. This assumption is made because that was the practice in the early church (see, for example, Acts 2:42 or 20:7). This practice was affirmed as standard by the Lutheran Confessions (Article XXIV of the Apology of the Augsburg Confession). And this practice has been reaffirmed as regular by various assemblies of the Lutheran churches.

In preparing for the Lord's Day and the chief service of the week, the altar guild will see to it that the chancel and its furnishings are cleaned (and the nave, if that is part of their responsibility). The paraments proper for the day or season will be hung. If the altar guild has the responsibility of caring for the vestments of the congregation, the vestments for the minister and any assistants will be set out. The candles will be checked and, if necessary, changed. The vessels and linens for Holy Communion will be set up on the altar or credence (see chapter 13 for the arrangement of the sacramental vessels and linens). The missal stand will be put in its proper place. The lectionary will be placed on the lectern or reading desk.

In preparing for Holy Communion the altar guild will have to make sure that sufficient quantities of bread and wine are available. The bread may be individual *hosts*, an unleavened type of bread. Some churches prefer ordinary bread, the leavened type, which is set on the altar or credence as a single loaf. The symbolism of the single loaf is appropriate ("one loaf … one body" [1 Corinthians 10:17]), but breaking it up for the communicants can leave a messy array of crumbs on the altar. With either individual hosts or a single loaf, the appropriate sacred vessel will be needed. Individual hosts can be placed on the paten or in the pyx or ciborium. A single loaf will ordinarily be too large for these vessels, so a large paten or suitable tray will have to be used.

The flagon will have to be large enough to hold a sufficient amount of wine. If necessary, more than one flagon may be needed. The wine will be grape wine, but it may be either red or white. A sacramental or kosher wine should be used, since these do not contain any artificial preservatives. What should not be used are cheap, sparkling wines or wines made from fruits other than grapes. By no means should grape juice be used, since it is not wine. With regard to those persons who cannot drink wine for medical or other reasons, how to administer the Sacrament should be left to the discretion of the pastor.

Optional arrangements may also have to be taken care of. If there are flowers, they may have to be picked up from the florist or received from the florist when delivered. The altar guild will see to it that they are in the proper vases and stands. It may be advisable to leave the flowers in a cool place until shortly before the service begins. If there are festal or seasonal banners, they will have to be cleaned and hung. When a procession is going to be conducted, the processional cross, torches, and possibly censer will have to be brought out and made ready.

Most of the above preparations can be done ahead of time, that is, on the day before. A few items, such as placing the flowers or filling the flagon with wine, may have to be done shortly before the service. How long ahead of time these things need to be done will depend on local circumstances. In any event, the work of the altar guild should be completed in a way that does not interfere with the preparations that the minister(s) must make before the service.[1]

After the service the altar guild will attend to the necessary cleanup. The vessels and linens can be cleaned as described earlier in chapters 12 and 13. If any of the Lord's body and blood remain, they can be disposed of in a number of ways. The best way is to consume the remaining elements, since the Lord said, "Take and eat. … Take and drink," and did not provide for anything that was left over. There is historic precedent for reserving the remaining elements against the next communion. The hosts can be stored in a pyx or ciborium (apart from unconsecrated hosts), the blood of the Lord in a suitable cruet or flagon (apart from unconsecrated wine). What remains in the chalice, however, should either be consumed or poured into the piscina or onto the ground, since there may be crumbs or other foreign matter in it. The reserved elements may then be kept in the sacristy or placed on the altar or credence and covered with a white veil. It is un-Lutheran and irreverent to place unused elements in the trash or to pour the remainder of what is in the chalice or flagon into the common drain.

A few other items may also be necessary for the altar guild to do after the service. The missal stand and book may be removed from the altar and placed in the sacristy. Items used in the procession will have to be cleaned and put away. If there are flowers, they should be dispersed according to congregational custom (either to those who paid for them or, better, to the sick or shut-in); they should not be left in the church. The chancel should be left clean, so any obvious dirt or stains should be cleaned up.

At one time in the history of the church the Sacrament of Holy Baptism was administered in a ceremony apart from the Divine Service. Because the Sacrament is a public and official act of the church, however, it should be conducted in the chief and public service of the church. The liturgical revisions of the 1960s and the service books of the church both indicate that Baptism should be administered in the chief service of the congregation. Only under extraordinary circumstances should the Sacrament be conducted at other times. The *Agenda* directs that Holy Baptism be celebrated in the Divine Service at the beginning of the service, immediately after the opening hymn.[2]

When Baptism is administered before or after the Easter season, the paschal candle may be moved from its position near the altar to a place near the font (this should be done before the service begins). If the baptismal font does not have running water, it should be filled shortly before or immediately after the opening hymn. If a baptismal shell is used to administer the water, it should be placed near the font with the necessary napkin and towel. If other accessories are used, such as a chrisom or candle, they may also be placed near the font. When there is no convenient place, these items may be placed on a tray and held by an assistant.

After the service in which there is a Baptism, the altar guild will have to empty and dry the bowl of the baptismal font if it does not have running water. The water from the Baptism should be poured into the piscina or onto the ground. Any linens used that the congregation retains will have to be laundered.

The Offices

The Offices are daily prayer services in which Holy Communion is not celebrated. In the Lutheran tradition there are two offices, Matins and Vespers, also known as Morning Prayer and Evening Prayer.[3] The origin and development of these offices are complex, but they seem to go back to the Old Testament practice of having fixed times for prayer in the morning and the evening.[4]

In contrast to the Divine Service the Offices are quite simple. They center around psalmody and hymns, the reading of Scripture and its exposition, and prayer. The altar, pulpit, and lectern are vested in the paraments for the season. The office lights are used or, if the chancel arrangement allows, a torch is positioned near the lectern (or two torches flank the lectern).

Other appointments may be readied according to local custom. The themes of light and new beginning in Morning Prayer make the visibility of the baptismal font appropriate. It may be filled with water and set in a prominent place (or if fixed, the assembly may gather in a place near the font). For Evening Prayer the use of incense may be appropriate. The psalmody for Evening Prayer begins with a verse from Psalm 141, "Let my prayer rise before you as incense" (this verse is the antiphon before the canticle in Vespers as well). Since the theme of light is prominent in Evening Prayer, a large candle may be placed before the assembly also.

In *Lutheran Worship* a third office is provided, the Office of Compline. This service is for later in the evening, at the close of day. This service is simple and requires only the book from which the lesson is to be read and the candles.

Although daily prayer is not prominent in the life of most congregations today, it was never intended by the Lutheran reformers that this aspect of the church's life be discontinued. The church needs to pray, publicly as well as privately, not just on Sunday but throughout the week. It is encouraging that this practice is being restored in more and more congregations. Hopefully it will become the norm in Lutheran church life.

Occasional Services

Occasional services are, by definition, services which are conducted in addition to the regular services of the church year (Sundays and festivals) and daily prayer offices. They are for specific occasions in the lives of individual church members, but they also involve the life of the congregation as a whole.

The Order for *Marriage* is a service of worship and therefore its focus is not on the bridal couple but on God. The service offers praise to God for his institution of marriage and asks for his blessing on the couple being married. Anything that distracts from this principle should not be allowed. Traditionally weddings were not performed during the penitential seasons of Advent and Lent, but more latitude is allowed today. They should not, however, be done on Ash Wednesday or during Holy Week.

Many wedding couples and their families take the arrangements of the service into their own hands and do much of the work, but the responsibility for overseeing the arrangements still lies with the altar guild. The paraments are those of the season and are not coordinated with the colors of the wedding. Flowers and other decorations must be handled within the guidelines of this manual, and not all florists are familiar with them. In addition to the regular appointments a kneeling cushion for the bride and groom may be used. Most congregations have one of these in their possession. A recent innovation is the so-called "unity candle." The theological symbolism is vague, since the two do become "one" flesh but the "two" individuals do not cease to exist. The action involved in the lighting of this candle is a sentimentality that distracts from the real action of God's uniting the two into one. For these reasons the unity candle has no place in a Christian wedding service.

Sometimes there is a request for the wedding service to include the celebration of Holy Communion. From a pastoral perspective this is inappropriate, since many of the attendants and guests at the service are probably not members of the congregation and are therefore strangers to the pastor and not under his pastoral care. From a confessional perspective it is also inappropriate, since many of these same people may come from a different confessional background. The altar guild, therefore, should not be called to prepare the chancel for Holy Communion.

After the wedding service the altar guild is responsible for cleaning the chancel and getting it ready for the next service. Members of the families of the married couple may offer to help clean the church. If they do, the work should still remain under the supervision of the altar guild.

The Order for the *Burial of the Dead* or funeral is another type of occasional service. The service included in *Lutheran Worship Agenda* indicates the kind of assistance that the altar guild may be called on to perform.[5] When the funeral coach arrives from the mortuary, the coffin is met in the narthex by the pastor (and assistants). Here the funeral pall is placed over the coffin and it is moved to the front of the nave. The processional cross and the paschal candle or torches may be used in this procession and put into position next to the coffin. Flower arrangements may be put on the gradine or on flower stands, but they should not be too large or numerous that they distract from the altar. The paraments are those for the season of the church year. As with the wedding service it is usually inadvisable to include the celebration of Holy Communion.

After the funeral service the altar guild will see to it that the church is ready for the next service. The funeral pall must be put away. Flowers and flower stands have to be removed. The paschal candle or torches will be returned to their places.

The rite of *confirmation* is technically not an occasional service but a rite set within the Divine Service. Nevertheless, it is not a regular part of the church's weekly worship and may require some additional work by the altar guild. If the confirmands do not kneel at the chancel rail, a special place may have to be arranged. Useful for this part of the rite is the litany or prayer desk, also called a prie dieu. Some congregations have the custom of using special confirmation gowns for the confirmands. Unfortunately, most of the gowns that can be rented or bought are academic in character and therefore not fitting for a churchly rite. The altar guild could make a white capelike garment or have them made, or they could invest in a set of simple and inexpensive albs. Or the congregation could dispense with the gown tradition entirely. None of the other rites in which an individual lay person of the congregation participates (Baptism, Communion, marriage, burial) requires a special robe or garment.

The *Confessional Service*, as envisioned in the *Agenda*, is a service intended for use apart from the Divine Service.[6] The chancel will be arranged as for the Divine Service, except that the Sacramental vessels and linens are not set up. If the confessional service is scheduled as part of the Day of Supplication and Prayer, the paraments may be changed to purple. The penitents may come up individually to the altar rail, or a prayer desk or prie dieu may be provided at the head of the nave. These same arrangements may be made for a regularly scheduled "Individual Confession and Absolution" if this rite is conducted in the chancel.[7]

Seasonal Services

Many Lutheran churches hold special midweek services during the seasons of Advent and Lent. These services are usually of the simple prayer type, such as Vespers or Evening Prayer. Preparations for them will not be elaborate. They will be similar to the preparations made for the evening offices. Because they are additional services, however, the altar guild will have extra work to do during these seasons.

Notes

1. See Appendix B, which is a summary list of things to check and do before the service. See also Appendix C, which is a list of things to do after the service.

2. *Lutheran Worship Agenda* (St. Louis: Concordia Publishing House, 1984), p. 98.

3. *Lutheran Worship* provides an order for each of these four offices. There are different elements in each and slightly different themes.

4. For a more detailed explanation of these services see John T. Pless, "Daily Prayer," in *Lutheran Worship: History and Practice*, ed. by Fred L. Precht (St. Louis: Concordia Publishing House, 1993), pp. 440–70.

5. See the "Notes" for the service on p. 196.

6. *Agenda*, p. 140.

7. See the *Agenda*, p. 144.

A

Devotions and Prayers[1]

Devotions

A simple devotion such as the following may open the altar guild meeting. If possible, the devotion should be held in the church before the altar guild goes to its meeting place.

An appropriate hymn may be sung.

L: In the name of the Father and of the ✠ Son and of the Holy Spirit.

R: Amen

L: Make haste, O God, to deliver me;

R: make haste to help me, O Lord.

All: Glory be to the Father and to the Son

      and to the Holy Spirit;

   as it was in the beginning,

      is now, and will be forever. Amen

Psalm 1, 15, 101, or 112 may be said. The following antiphon may be spoken before the psalm and after the Gloria Patri.

You who fear [the LORD], trust in the LORD—he is their help and their shield.

A seasonal or otherwise appropriate reading from Scripture may be read.

A suitable collect from those given below may be prayed.

The Meeting

After the meeting a suitable collect from those given below may be prayed, and then all may pray the Lord's Prayer.

In place of the above devotion, the Order of Matins/Morning Prayer or Vespers/Evening Prayer may be used, depending on the time of day.

Collects for before a Meeting

Direct us, O Lord, in all our doings with your most gracious favor, and further us with your continual help, that in all our works begun, continued, and ended in you we may glorify your holy name and finally by your mercy obtain everlasting life; through Jesus Christ, your Son, our Lord, who lives and reigns with you and the Holy Spirit, one God, now and forever.

R: Amen

Grant, we beseech you, merciful Lord, to your faithful people pardon and peace, that they may be cleansed from all their sins and serve you with a quiet mind; through Jesus Christ, your Son, our Lord, who lives and reigns with you and the Holy Spirit, one God, now and forever.

R: Amen

Almighty God, grant, we beseech you, that we may handle holy things with reverence and perform our work with such faithfulness and devotion that it may be acceptable to you and obtain your blessings; through Jesus Christ, your Son, our Lord, who lives and reigns with you and the Holy Spirit, one God, now and forever.

R: Amen

Blessed Lord Jesus, who loved your Father's house, help us to love your service and your church, that as Solomon was taught to build and adorn your temple, so we, to whom has been committed here the care of your altar and sanctuary, may perform our holy work with pure hearts and hands; who lives and reigns with the Father and the Holy Spirit, one God, now and forever.

R: Amen

Collects for after a Meeting

Grant us, we beseech you, almighty God, a steadfast faith in Jesus Christ, a cheerful hope in your mercy, and a sincere love to you and toward one another; through the same Jesus Christ, your Son, our Lord, who lives and reigns with you and the Holy Spirit, one God, now and forever.

R: Amen

O God, through the grace of your Holy Spirit you pour the gifts of love into the hearts of your faithful people. Grant to your servants health, both of mind and of body, that they may love you with their whole strength, and with their whole heart perform those things which are pleasing to you; through Jesus Christ, your Son, our Lord, who lives and reigns with you and the Holy Spirit, one God, now and forever.

R: Amen

Almighty God, who gave your only Son to be for us both a sacrifice for sin and an example of godly life, give us grace that we may always most thankfully receive this, his boundless benefit, and daily try to follow the blessed steps of his most holy life; through the same Jesus Christ, who lives and reigns with you and the Holy Spirit, one God, now and forever.

R: Amen

To God the Father who loved us and made us acceptable in the Beloved; to God the Son who loved us and freed us from our sins by his own blood; to God the Holy Spirit who pours out the love of God into our hearts: to the one true God be all love and all glory for time and for eternity.

R: Amen

To him who is able to keep us from falling and to present us faultless before the presence of his glory with great joy: to the only wise God, our Savior, be glory and majesty, dominion and power, now and always and forever and ever.

R: Amen

Private Prayers before and after Work

"Who may ascend the hill of the Lord? Who may stand in his holy place? He who has clean hands and a pure heart" (Psalm 24:3–4).

Almighty God, to whom all hearts are open, all desires known, and from whom no secrets are hidden, cleanse the thoughts of our hearts by the inspiration of your Holy Spirit, that we may perfectly love you and worthily magnify your holy name; through Jesus Christ, your Son, our Lord, who lives and reigns with you and the Holy Spirit, one God, now and forever. Amen

"He has filled them with skill to do all kinds of work as craftsmen, designers, embroiderers in blue, purple and scarlet yarn and fine linen, and weavers—all of them master craftsmen and designers" (Exodus 35:35).

Lord Jesus Christ, who accepted the service of faithful people during your earthly life, accept and bless the work of my hands in the care of your sanctuary, granting me a spirit of reverence for your house and worship, and preserving my soul and body as a living temple of your presence; to whom with the Father and the Holy Spirit be all honor and glory, now and forever. Amen

"Whatever is true, whatever is noble, whatever is right, whatever is pure, whatever is lovely, whatever is admirable—if anything is excellent or praiseworthy—think about such things" (Philippians 4:8).

Grant me, I beseech you, almighty and most merciful God, to desire fervently all things that are pleasing to you; and in everything you require me to do, grant me the knowledge, the will, and the ability to do it as I ought, to the glory of your holy name; through Jesus Christ, your Son, our Lord, who lives and reigns with you and the Holy Spirit, one God, now and forever. Amen

Almighty God, grant that I may handle holy things with reverence and that I may perform my work with such faithfulness and devotion that it may be acceptable to you and receive your blessings; through Jesus Christ, your Son, our Lord. Amen

God, accept and bless the work of my hands and all who serve you in the care and adornment of your sanctuary, that your holy name may be glorified; through Jesus Christ, your Son, our Lord. Amen

O Lord, our God, quicken my heart. Let me serve you in all humility. Let me serve you in all reverence. Let me serve you in all obedience. Give me a clean heart. Give me clean hands. Give me clean thoughts. Through Jesus Christ, our Lord. Amen

Notes

1. The devotions and prayers in this section have been revised from Chapter IV in Paul H. D. Lang, *What an Altar Guild Should Know* (St. Louis: Concordia Publishing House, 1964).

B
Guidelines for before the Service

Pray

Discern the time
- It is either the observance of a season of the church year or the celebration of a holy day. The calendar for the church year is located in front of the hymnal (*Lutheran Worship*, pp. 8–9; *The Lutheran Hymnal*, p. 3).
- Having discerned the time and nature of the day, the color is determined according to the calendar.

Clean the chancel

Arrange the furniture
- Depending on the service, the chancel furniture may have to be moved, such as the baptismal font or the paschal candle stand.

Check the paraments and linens
- If the season or festival has changed, locate the appropriate paraments (if they are different) and put them in place.
- If the fair linen is dirty, it must be replaced and/or laundered.

Check the candles

Put out flowers, banners, and other decorations if appointed

Put the missal stand and altar book on the altar, the lectionary on the lectern

Prepare for Holy Communion
- Put enough hosts in the pyx and a celebrant's host on the paten
- Put wine in the flagon or cruet, if individual glasses are used, fill them
- Put corporal on the altar, vest the chalice and place on corporal
- Put pyx and flagon on the altar, also individual glass trays if used
- Put extra purificators on the corporal
- If a credence is used: put corporal and purificators in burse; vest the chalice and put on credence; put pyx, flagon, and individual glass trays on credence

Prepare for Holy Baptism

- Put napkin and towel on/near font (or on a tray)
- If candle, baptismal garment, or other accessories are used, put them on/near the font (or on the tray)
- Place paschal candle near the font
- Fill font with warm water

Other preparations

- Get processional cross out and put in place
- Check torches and put in place
- Get thurible and boat ready (do not light coals until 10 or 15 minutes before the service)

C

Guidelines for after the Service

Clean the chancel

After Holy Communion
- Remove the communion vessels and linens to the sacristy
- Remove the missal stand and altar book to the sacristy
- Consume remaining elements OR put the consecrated hosts into the proper receptacle (not mixing them with unconsecrated hosts); put consecrated wine from flagon or cruet (or remaining individual glasses) into the proper receptacle (not mixing it with unconsecrated wine); pour remaining wine from chalice into the piscina or onto the ground
- Pour water into flagon/cruet, chalice, and the used individual glasses and then rinse out into the piscina or onto the ground
- Clean sacramental vessels and put in proper storage place
- Launder sacramental linens (this may be done at home)

After Holy Baptism
- Dispose of water from font by pouring it into the piscina or onto the ground
- Dry font bowl and put back in place
- Launder the linens

Other items
- Put processional cross and torches back in their proper places
- Safely dispose of coals from thurible and put thurible and boat in their place

Talk to the Pastor
- or the Altar Guild director, or leave one of them a note, if there are any questions about the next service

Pray
- Give thanks to God for this opportunity to serve

D

A Note on Communion Ware and Hygiene

The use of the chalice (or "common cup") used to be universal in Lutheranism but in the last century its use has become infrequent. One of the reasons for replacing it with "individual glasses" was hygiene. People believe (mistakenly) that germs are easily transmitted by using the chalice. However, the combination of the noble metal of the chalice (such as gold or silver) and the alcohol content of the wine makes the possibility for germs to be transmitted almost nonexistent. The following article explains this further:

> Can I get sick from using the common cup? No! The use of the common cup was traditional in all Christian churches until this century and was eliminated because of fears about sanitary matters concerning the transmission of disease. The question about disease transmission is answered best by the scientific community. A thorough study on the use of the common cup was done by professors Burroughs and Hemmers in 1965 and was reported in the Journal of Infectious Diseases. Their conclusion was:
>
>> Experiments on the transmission of organisms from one person to another by common use of the chalice showed that 0.001% of the organisms transferred even under the most favorable conditions and when conditions approximated those of actual use, no transmission could be detected.
>
> Recent concerns about the transmission of AIDS confirm this study. Dr. David Ho in the New England Journal of Medicine (December 1985) provided documentation that verified that there was no spread of the AIDS virus in saliva through common eating or drinking utensils. In effect, AIDS is spread only through sexual contact or the exchange of blood. No case of AIDS victims studied to date has shown any possibility of communicating the disease through saliva. Concerns about the chalice and AIDS are motivated more by fear than by scientific research, since no scientific research exists to connect the two.
>
> It is through hands that most disease is transmitted, which makes Communion by intinction more prone to disease than receiving the common cup, since those who give the Sacrament touch both the Host and Wine. And how many hands touch the "little glasses"? The alternative is to reject the command of Christ and refrain from Communion altogether.

Lutherans should remember that Martin Luther restored the cup when Roman Catholics had all but eliminated it from the peoples' Communion. He did it because his loyalty was to the command of Christ in the Bible. The use of the common cup was normative until the late nineteenth century and was eliminated in those churches in which Communion was not understood as being the Body and Blood of Christ.

Some Lutherans allow other methods of distribution, believing that the method of distribution does not matter. However, the use of the common chalice retains that which Our Lord indicated was His desire. And, its effect, where used, is to transmit not only salvation but also the oneness that comes from sharing the Blood of Christ from the Chalice in common with one's sisters and brothers. All the faithful respond to Christ's words: **"Then he took a cup, and when he had returned thanks, he gave it to them. 'Drink all of you from this,' he said."** (St. Matthew 26:27, Jerusalem Bible).[1]

Notes

1. "The Common Cup and Disease," reprinted from *The Bride of Christ*, vol XII, no. 3, copyright © 1988 by Lutheran Liturgical Renewal, Inc. Used by permission.

E

Glossary

Note: The words given in bold-face type are included in this glossary. See their definitions for additional information.

Absolution: In a general sense the forgiveness of sins. In a specific sense the forgiveness of sins which the pastor pronounces after the confession of sins at the beginning of the **Divine Service,** in the Service of Corporate Confession, or in private confession. See also **Sacrament.**

Acolyte: From a Greek word meaning "follower." Originally a person who "followed" the priest and assisted him with various duties. Today the term is understood to refer to the young persons who light and extinguish the candles, although it could refer to a person of any age who assists in any number of liturgical functions. See also **server.**

Adiaphoron: A Greek word meaning "indifferent." In matters of practice it refers to something that is neither commanded nor forbidden in Scripture, and the church has the freedom to decide how to do something. For example, the color of wine used in Holy Communion is not prescribed. The church is free to use either red wine or white wine. At times, however, it may be a matter of confession to do something in a particular way. If someone demanded that red wine be used, the congregation may decide to use only white wine to show that the indifferent matter of the wine's color cannot be made into an issue that is legalistically binding. The plural of adiaphoron is "adiaphora."

Advent: A season of the **church year** in the Time of Christmas. Advent is a season of preparation in repentant hope and anticipation of Christ's coming (his first and second). There are four Sundays in Advent. The **liturgical color** is purple or blue.

Agenda: A service book containing the orders of the rites and services of the church.

Alb: A **vestment** worn by the minister and the liturgical assistants. It is a long, white garment with long sleeves. The alb is the proper vestment for the celebration of **Holy Communion.**

Ambo: Raised platform for reading or preaching; today often used as another term for **pulpit** or reading desk.

Altar: The most important piece of liturgical furniture and the focal point of the worship space. The altar symbolizes the presence of God. Its function is sacramental and sacrificial. The sacramental function is that it is where God gives his people the gifts of Christ's sacrifice, namely, in the Lord's Supper. The sacrificial function means that it is where the congregation offers its prayer, praise, and thanksgiving in response to God's gifts. The altar may either be fixed to the **east** wall of the **chancel** or be freestanding.

Altar book: A service book containing the liturgy of the **Divine Service** and the **propers.**

Altar rail: A rail or low fence which separates the **sanctuary** from the **choir** or the **chancel** from the **nave.** In many churches the communicants kneel at the altar rail to receive Holy Communion or Absolution. Also known as a chancel rail or communion rail.

Antependium: A **parament** which hangs from the pulpit or lectern and displays the color of the season. Also known as a pulpit or lectern fall, or a pulpit or lectern frontal. The plural is "antependia."

Ascension: A **major festival** of the church year which occurs 40 days after Easter (always on a Thursday). It commemorates the ascension of our Lord into heaven (see Acts 1:1–11). The **liturgical color** is white.

Ash Wednesday: A **major festival** which marks the beginning of **Lent** and falls 40 days before Easter, not counting Sundays. Its name originated from the medieval custom of imposing ashes on the foreheads of the penitent. The **liturgical color** is purple or black.

Assisting minister: In a general sense this term refers to any person who assists in any part of the service. According to the rubrics of *Lutheran Worship*, the word designates a person who conducts certain portions of the liturgy (those parts not reserved for the **presiding minister**), reads the Old Testament and Epistle, and distributes the blood of our Lord. The assisting minister can be either an ordained clergyman or a layperson. See also **lector** and **server**.

Baptism, Holy: A **rite** in which water is applied according to God's command and combined with God's Word. Through the work of the Holy Spirit the person being baptized is united with Christ and receives the forgiveness of sins and new life. Infants are baptized and then instructed in the faith, while adults are instructed in the faith and then baptized. See also **Sacrament.**

Baptism of Our Lord: A festival which falls on the Sunday after the **Epiphany of Our Lord,** commemorating our Lord's Baptism in the Jordan River by John the Baptist. The **liturgical color** for this festival is white.

Baptismal shell: A real shell or a shell made of precious metal used to apply the water in Holy Baptism.

Baptismal towel: A piece of white cloth that is used to wipe the head of the baptismal candidate or dry the hands of the pastor. Also known as a napkin.

Baptistery: In centuries past and in some traditions today, a separate building or room in the church building where the Sacrament of Holy Baptism was/is administered.

Black gown: See **pulpit gown.**

Bread: See **elements.**

Burial of the Dead: A service to commemorate the death of a Christian and the interment of his or her body. It is proper that a baptized Christian be buried from the church. If the person had to be interred ahead of time or if his or her body was cremated, this service can be used as a memorial service. See also **procession** and **rite.**

Burse: An envelopelike case which is used to hold the **corporal, Post-Communion veil,** and **purificators.** The cloth covering is of the same material and the same color as the **paraments.**

Canonical hours: The services of the daily prayer of the church. Also called an **office.** Historically there were eight offices conducted at three hour intervals over a 24-hour period: Matins, Lauds, Prime, Terce, Sext, Nones, Vespers, and Compline. The Lutheran Reformers retained two of these offices: **Matins** and **Vespers.** *Lutheran Worship* includes a third, **Compline,** also called "Prayer at the Close of Day."

Cassock: A long, close-fitting, black **vestment** with long sleeves over which the **surplice** is worn. Historically it was the everyday attire of the clergy.

Celebrant: See **presiding minister.**

Celebrant's host: A communion bread larger than the breads distributed to the communicants. The standard size is 2¾ inches in diameter. Its larger size makes it more visible to the congregation during the elevation. This host is placed on the **paten** when the chalice is vested.

Censer: See **thurible.**

Cerecloth: A protector linen that is placed on the **mensa** of the altar. Originally it was treated with wax to protect the **fair linen** from the dampness of the altar.

Cere linen: See **cerecloth.**

Ceremony: Technically the *actions* in worship as opposed to the *words.* See also **liturgy** and **rite.** Popularly understood as synonymous with **rite.**

Chalice: A cup with a bowl, stem, and foot that is used to distribute the Lord's blood. Also referred to as the common cup.

Chalice pall: A 7–9 inch square of glass, metal, or plastic covered with white material. It fits over the **paten** when the chalice is vested.

Chalice veil: An 18–24 inch square cloth of the same material and of the same color as the **paraments.** It is the last item draped over the vested chalice. See also **Post-Communion veil.**

Chancel: One of the two main divisions of the worship space. It is the part of the building where the altar is located, that is, on its actual or so-called liturgical **east** end. In most churches the chancel is one or two steps higher than the **nave.** See also **choir** and **sanctuary.**

Chancel rail: See **altar rail.**

Chasuble: A poncholike **vestment** which fits over the alb. Like the paraments, it reflects the **liturgical** color of the season. It is properly worn by the **presiding minister** at services which include the Lord's Supper.

Choir: Popularly understood as the group of singers who assist with the liturgy and the congregation's singing. Architecturally, it is the part of the **chancel** closest to the **nave,** since that is where the liturgical singers historically sat.

Chrism: A consecrated and usually fragranced oil applied in the administration of Holy Baptism, symbolizing the sealing of the Holy Spirit.

Chrismon: A white-colored symbol of Christ or his nativity made from wood or Styrofoam and used to decorate the Christmas tree.

Chrisom: A white garment worn by a candidate for Holy Baptism symbolizing the righteousness of Christ conferred in the Sacrament.

Christ the King Sunday: The last Sunday of the **church year** pointing to the second coming of Christ when he visibly manifests his universal reign. An option to the Sunday of the Fulfillment.

Christmas: See the **Nativity of Our Lord.**

Church year: The liturgical organization of the year in which the great acts that God has done in Christ for our salvation are celebrated. One aspect of the church year is called the *temporale,* the structure of the year according to the Christological festivals. This year can be divided into three "times": The Time of Christmas, the Time of Easter, and the Time of the Church. Each time can be subdivided into "seasons." The Time of Christmas includes the season of **Advent, Christmas** and its season, and **Epiphany** and its season. The Time of Easter consists of the season of **Lent, Holy Week,** and **Easter** and its season. The Time of the Church begins with the **Holy Trinity** and includes all of the following Sundays, enumerated as Sundays after **Pentecost,** until the last Sunday of the church year, the Sunday of the Fulfillment. As the civil year has its beginning on January 1, so the church year has its start on the First Sunday in **Advent.** During the course of this liturgical year the church commemorates the events of the life of Christ (the Time of Christmas and the Time of Easter) and meditates on his teaching and its application to the life of the church (the Time of the Church).

The other aspect of the church year is called the *sanctorale*, a cycle of commemorations of the saints, martyrs, and certain events in the life of the church. While dating in the *temporale* depends on the dates of the First Sunday in Advent and of Easter, the festivals of the *sanctorale* are on the same dates every calendar year. See also **major festivals** and **minor festivals.**

Ciborium: A sacramental vessel shaped like a **chalice** but having a cover. It was used originally as a container for consecrated **hosts.** It now can also function either as a **pyx** or a **paten.**

Cincture: A rope or band of cloth fastened around the waist to secure an **alb.**

Collect: As one of the **propers,** a brief prayer which brings together the theme of a season or festival. This prayer is the Collect of the Day. There are other collects which are not tied to a season or festival but still bring together a certain theme or thought, such as "The Collect for the Church" (*Lutheran Worship,* p. 156; *The Lutheran Hymnal,* p. 14) or "The Collect for Peace" (*Lutheran Worship,* p. 234; *The Lutheran Hymnal,* p. 45).

Color, liturgical: See **liturgical color.**

Communion, Holy: The true body and blood of our Lord Jesus Christ given to Christians to eat and drink. In the **rite** the earthly elements of bread and wine are consecrated by the **presiding minister** and are given to Christians for the forgiveness of sins and the strengthening of their faith. Also called the Lord's Supper or the Eucharist. See also **Sacrament.**

Communion rail: See **altar rail.**

Compline: One of the **canonical hours** now called "Prayer at the Close of Day." The mood of this **office** is serene, and the theme of its prayer is indicated in the opening versicle: "The Lord Almighty grant us a quiet night and peace at the last."

Confirmation: A **rite** in which a person instructed in the Christian faith, trusting in the promise given in **Holy Baptism,** publicly confesses the doctrine which he or she has been taught and publicly pledges to remain faithful to God and his Word and to be faithful in the use of God's Word and the Sacraments.

Cope: A long, capelike **vestment** open in the front and fastened with a clasp. It is worn when the minister must go outside or for conducting one of the **offices.**

Corporal: An 18–21 inch square, white sacramental linen. It is placed in the center of the **altar** and on it the vessels for Holy Communion are set.

Corpus: A carved figure of the crucified Christ. When the corpus is attached to the cross, the cross is called a **crucifix.**

Cotta: A white **vestment** that is worn over the cassock. It is similar to a **surplice,** except that its length is shorter and the sleeves are shorter. Usually worn by **servers,** the organist, and choir.

Credence: A table or shelf on the **south** wall of the chancel to hold the sacramental vessels and linens, service books, **incense boat,** and other liturgical accessories.

Credence linen: A white cloth similar to the **fair linen** to cover the **credence.**

Cross: (1) As a verb, it refers to the action of making the sign of the cross on oneself as a remembrance of Holy Baptism. To make the sign of the cross, hold the small finger and thumb together, extending the three remaining fingers, and with the tips of these three fingers touch the forehead, the chest, then the left shoulder, then the right shoulder. (2) As a noun, it refers to the instrument which was used to crucify the Savior and the place where he won our redemption. As a symbol of the Christian faith, it signifies the salvation we have in Christ. There are several uses of the cross in a liturgical setting: the altar cross (preferably a **crucifix**), which sits on the **gradine** of the altar, on the altar itself, or is suspended over the altar; the **pectoral cross,** which is worn on a chain around the neck; and the **processional cross** or crucifix, which is carried in **processions.**

Crucifer: The liturgical assistant or **server** who carries the **processional cross** or crucifix.

Crucifix: A **cross** which has a **corpus** attached to it. In the early church a plain **cross** was used. The crucifix was a medieval product when the suffering of Christ received increasing emphasis. From a Lutheran standpoint the crucifix, because of its incarnational implications, is preferable.

Cruet: A container of glass or precious metal for wine or water in the Communion service. It is often smaller than the **flagon.**

Daily prayer: See **office.**

Deacon: From a New Testament Greek word simply meaning "servant." The Latin equivalent of deacon is *minister.* In the early church they seem to have been the lowest rank of the threefold order of ordained clergymen: deacon, presbyter (priest), and bishop. Later on many of the deacon's functions were taken over by the presbyter, or priest. In the modern church there is a broad application of different functions to the office of deacon. In a general sense, the deacon is someone who assists the pastor in his duties. In some churches these duties include preaching and administering the sacraments; in others, deacons function as lay **assisting ministers;** and yet in others their work centers on caring for the sick, the poor, the homebound.

Divine Service: The service of Word and Sacrament, the chief weekly service of the parish. This was the practice of the early church and was affirmed as standard by the **Lutheran Confessions.** The custom of having the Sunday service be simply a Service of the Word without Communion was a late development that worked its way into the Lutheran church as a result of **Pietism** and the Reformed churches, among whom the sermon was elevated and the Sacraments devalued. The term *Divine Service* comes by way of the German *Gottesdienst,* which literally means "God's service" or "service of God." Foremost is the idea that it is God serving those whom he has gathered in Word and Sacrament. Secondary is the idea that those who are gathered are serving God (worship). Divine Service, therefore, is a more appropriate term for Lutherans to use than "worship" or "worship service." See also **liturgy, office,** and **occasional service.**

Dorsal: See **dossal.**

Dossal: An ornamental cloth hung behind the altar from a rod, coordinating with or sometimes matching the color of the **paraments.** Used in place of a **reredos.**

East: A reference to the direction within the church building. Traditionally, a church was built on an east-west axis, with the altar at the east end and the **narthex** at the west end. As one faced the altar, then, the left was north and the right was south. Although this tradition is no longer held to in building churches, it is still customary to refer to the altar end as liturgical *east,* the narthex end as liturgical *west,* the left as liturgical *north,* and the right as liturgical *south.* Liturgical north is sometimes called the *Gospel side* and liturgical south the *Epistle side.*

Easter: See **Resurrection of Our Lord.**

Easter Vigil: See the **Vigil of Easter.**

Elements: The visible materials used in the **sacraments.** In **Holy Baptism** the element is water. In **Holy Communion** the elements are bread and wine. See **Sacrament.**

Entrance rite: See **procession.**

Epiphany of Our Lord: One of the **major festivals** of the **church year,** falling on January 6. The Epiphany, in Western church tradition, commemorates the visit of the Wise

Men to the infant Jesus in Bethlehem. The theme of Epiphany and its season is the manifestation or revelation of the incarnate God to the world. The **liturgical color** is white.

Epistle side: See **south.**

Eternal light: See **sanctuary light.**

Eucharist: From a Greek word meaning "thanksgiving." See **Communion, Holy.**

Eucharistic lights: The two candles on the **altar** or **gradine** that are lighted for the **Divine Service.** However, these two candles may/should be lighted even when Holy Communion is not celebrated.

Evening Prayer: See **Vespers.**

Ewer: A pitcher of precious metal that is used to bring water to the baptismal **font.**

Fair linen: A cloth of fine linen that is placed on top of the **mensa** of the altar. It is the last of the three cloths placed on the altar, on top of the **cerecloth** and the **frontal linen.**

Fall: See **antependium.**

Flagon: A covered sacramental vessel that looks like a pitcher and into which wine is poured for use in **Holy Communion.** See also **cruet.**

Font: An item of liturgical furniture which contains a bowl that holds water for use in **Holy Baptism.** Located in the **narthex,** in the **nave,** or at the head of the nave. In some churches the font is located in the **baptistery.** Not to be confused with "fount," which is a shortened form of "fountain."

Footpace: See **predella.**

Frontal: A **parament** that covers the front of the altar from end to end and from top to bottom. It is attached to a piece of cloth called a **frontal linen,** which holds it in place. See also **frontlet** and **superfrontal.**

Frontal linen: A piece of cloth attached to the **frontal** or **superfrontal.** The frontal linen is the exact size of the **mensa** and lies on top of the mensa to hold the frontal or superfrontal in place.

Frontlet: A **parament** made of a band of material 6–8 inches wide and 12–18 inches long. Instead of a **frontal** or **superfrontal,** two frontlets hang down the front of the altar, each about 12–18 inches from the end of the altar.

Funeral: See **Burial of the Dead.**

Funeral pall: A large piece of material 9–12 feet long and 6–8 feet wide used to cover the coffin and its carriage in the church building. Sometimes its color may coordinate with the **paraments,** but most often it is white and adorned with a simple cross or Christian symbol. It symbolizes the righteousness with which Christ covered the deceased at his or her Baptism.

Geneva gown: See **pulpit gown.**

Good Friday: A **major festival** of the **church year** on which the church remembers the crucifixion of Jesus. Good Friday is the most solemn day of the church year because the Man who was innocent of sin had to suffer and sorrow for all the sins of the world. The **liturgical color** is black.

Gospel book: A **lectionary** which contains only the readings of the Holy Gospel. This book is usually large and ornate so that it makes a fitting presentation when carried in **procession.**

Gospel procession: A **procession** into the middle of the **nave** for the reading of the Holy Gospel. The proceeding into the nave signifies that the Word become flesh is still present in the midst of his people. Ordinarily this procession is accompanied by **thurible** and **torches.**

Gospel side: See **east.**

Gradine: The back part of the **altar** which is raised above the **mensa.** With a freestanding altar, the gradine is a shelf on the **east** wall. With an altar fixed to the east wall, the gradine is the rear part of the altar. The gradine serves as a place on which to set the **eucharistic lights** (but not with a freestanding altar, then the candlesticks sit on the altar itself), the **altar cross,** and flower vases (if local custom permits). Also called a retable.

Holy Friday: Another name for **Good Friday.**

Holy Saturday: The day after **Good Friday.**

Holy Thursday: Another name for **Maundy Thursday.**

Holy Trinity: One of the **major festivals** of the **church year.** This festival observes the biblical doctrine of the Triune God, the God of the Old and New Testaments, the one and only true God. The proper preface for the day sounds the theme: "We worship the Trinity in person and the Unity in substance, of majesty coequal." The color for the day is white.

Holy Week: A season of the Time of Easter. Beginning with **Palm Sunday** the church remembers during Holy Week the final events of our Lord's earthly life which led up to his crucifixion. This week is the climax of the **church year** and with the Feast of the **Resurrection of Our Lord** is the center of the church's faith and life. See also **Maundy Thursday, Good Friday,** and **Triduum.**

Host: From the Latin *hostia*, which means "sacrifice, victim." A term used to designate the individual communion breads or wafers. Hosts are small, round, flat pieces of bread (standard size is 1⅛ to 1⅜ inches in diameter), sometimes impressed with a cross or other Christian symbol. See also **celebrant's host.**

Host box: See **pyx.**

Incense: A wood or resin which, when burned, gives off a sweet fragrance or aroma. Incense has a long history of use in the church and even predates the church in its use in religious rites. As an external in Christian worship, it has both sacramental and sacrificial symbolism. Sacramentally, incense symbolizes the mystery of God's coming to us, as in the cloud of glory which led the Israelites in the wilderness (Exodus 13:21; Numbers 9:17) and which filled the tabernacle and temple (Exodus 40:34; 1 Kings 8:11; Isaiah 6:1–4), and ultimately his coming in the glory of our Lord's becoming flesh (John 1:14). Sacrificially, incense represents our prayers, praises, and thanksgiving to God (Psalm 141:2). Unfortunately, the use of incense is often labeled "high church" or "Catholic," suggesting that there are only two alternatives in worship, namely, that the externals of worship are kept with little or no freedom of choice, or that ceremony is unimportant and can be disregarded or even held in contempt. The roots, however, of the use of incense are biblical. Incense belonged to the rites of the tabernacle and then of the temple in Jerusalem. Its use in Christianity was almost universal until the time of the Reformation. It was not Dr. Luther, however, who discontinued its use. Incense was thrown out by radicals who objected to any external aspects in worship. Among the many other things these radicals threw out were crosses, stained-glass windows, candles, and even music. See also **thurible** and **thurifer.**

Incense boat: A small bowl or dish, usually footed, which holds the **incense** ready to be put in the **thurible.**

Incense spoon: A spoon which is used to transfer the **incense** from the **incense boat** to the **thurible.**

Lavabo: A bowl of glass or precious metal which holds water that is used for the ceremonial washing of the **presiding minister's** fingers or hands. This washing takes place during the offertory.

Lavabo towel: A towel used to dry the fingers or hands of the **presiding minister** after he rinses them in the **lavabo.**

Lectern: A piece of liturgical furniture in addition to the **altar, pulpit,** and **font.** It is normally smaller than the pulpit and is located on the opposite side of the **chancel** on the same line that divides the chancel from the **nave.** It serves as the place from where the Scriptures are read. In some modern churches there is no lectern, since the pulpit serves as the place where the Scriptures are both read and expounded.

Lectionary: (1) The list of readings appointed for each Sunday and festival of the **church year.** (2) A service book containing those readings. At present, there are two lectionaries in use in the Lutheran church. One is the Three-Year Series, in which different sets of readings are appointed over three years designated as A, B, and C. This lectionary came into being as a result of the liturgical revisions of the 1960s. The other lectionary is the One-Year Series. This list is based on the traditional readings which developed in the course of the church's history.

Lector: An **assisting minister** who reads the first two readings, that is, the Old Testament and the Epistle.

Lent: A season of the **church year** which serves as a preparation for Easter. In the early church the emphasis during Lent was on preparation for Baptism, which would take place on the **Vigil of Easter.** Later on devout penitential practices were emphasized. Today Lent balances the themes of baptismal renewal and repentance. Lent begins with **Ash Wednesday** and ends with the Eve of **Palm Sunday.** The color for Lent is purple.

Lenten veil: Veils of unbleached linen or purple that are used to cover statues, pictures, and other ornamental objects during **Lent** as a sign of restraint and austerity during this penitential season.

Lights: A term used for the various candles employed in worship. See **eucharistic lights** and **office lights.** At first the use of lights was probably purely functional, namely, the minister and worshipers needed to see. But lights also have a symbolic purpose. They signify the presence of God and Christ as "the Light of the world."

Linens: A word used to designate the white-colored pieces of cloth used in the chancel. Originally these cloths were made of fine linen, but today a number of synthetic materials are available. The altar linens are the **cerecloth, credence linen, fair linen,** and **frontal linen.** The linens for Holy Communion are the **chalice pall, corporal,** and **purificator.** The baptismal linens are the **napkin** and the **towel.**

Liturgical color: Liturgical colors are used for **paraments, vestments,** and other accessories to signify the season of the **church year.** Color also has a symbolic meaning, that is, a particular color may evoke a certain emotion, such as love or purity. The five standard colors and their basic uses are as follows: white for festivals of Christ and saints who died a natural death, red for **Pentecost** and martyrs' days, purple for the preparatory seasons of **Advent** and **Lent,** black for **Ash Wednesday** and **Good Friday,** and green for **ordinary** or nonfestival times. Alternate colors are blue (for **Advent**), scarlet (for **Holy Week**), gold (for **Easter**).

Liturgy: In its broad and most basic sense, liturgy is the equivalent of **Divine Service.** This means that in the liturgy God gathers his people around Word and Sacrament and serves them with his gifts of the forgiveness of sins, life, and salvation. God's people, in turn, respond to God's generosity with their prayers, praises, and thanks. In the liturgy there are two roles: the role of the clergy and the role of the laity, or people. The clergy, particularly the **presiding minister,** speaks and acts for God in his place by proclaiming God's Word and administering the gifts of God in the **sacraments.** The laity, on the other hand, receive God's gifts and respond to them with prayer, praise, and thanksgiving. In its narrow sense, liturgy refers to the text (and music) of the Divine Service as it has evolved in the church and been handed down for two millennia. See also **ceremony** and **rite**.

Lutheran Confessions: Statements of belief and practice that were adopted by the Lutheran Reformers and others in the 16th century as their confessions of faith and life. These statements are the following: the Three Chief Symbols (Apostles' Creed, Nicene Creed, Athanasian Creed), the Augsburg Confession (1530), the Apology of the Augsburg Confession (1531), the Smalcald Articles (1537), the Treatise on the Power and Primacy of the Pope (1537), the Small Catechism of Dr. Martin Luther (1529), the Large Catechism of Dr. Martin Luther (1529), and the Formula of Concord (1577). It should be noted that the Augsburg Confession, the first of these confessional statements, was not a document drawn up to start a new church, but a confession that what the Lutheran party believes, teaches, and confesses was nothing else than what the church from the beginning has believed, taught, and confessed.

Major Festivals: Festivals which celebrate or commemorate the major events of Christ's work for the redemption of mankind. According to this definition the major festivals are the following: the **Nativity of Our Lord,** the **Epiphany of Our Lord,** the **Resurrection of Our Lord,** the **Ascension of Our Lord,** and **Pentecost.** Classified with these because of their importance are **Ash Wednesday, Palm Sunday, Maundy Thursday, Good Friday,** and the **Holy Trinity.** Because these are important festivals, their observance has precedence over any other day or observance. In the early centuries of the Lutheran church the highest festivals were recognized with a three-day observance. The high festivals of the church were Christmas, Easter, and Pentecost.

Marriage: An occasional service in which a man and a woman are united in marriage. The concern of the church (which does not have to perform the wedding ceremony in order for it to be valid) is to have the couple profess vows which conform to the biblical view of marriage and to ask God's blessing on this union of husband and wife. Because of the solemnity of **Ash Wednesday** and **Holy Week,** marriage services are not held at these times.

Mass: See **Divine Service.**

Matins: The morning weekday **office** of daily prayer. This office consists of a hymn, psalmody, a reading from Scripture, sermon, canticle, and prayers. Historically the sermon was not part of the daily prayer office, but with Luther's emphasis on the proclamation of the Word it has received a place in the Lutheran tradition of the office. Sometimes Matins is also called "Morning Prayer," although the two services can be distinct in theme and structure. See also **canonical hours.**

Maundy Thursday: A **major festival** of the **church year.** It is the Thursday before Easter, so its date is determined by the date of Easter. The term *maundy* comes from the Latin *mandatum*, which means "commandment." The day was called Maundy Thursday because it was on this night that Jesus said, "A new *command* I give you: Love one another" (John 13:34). This festival commemorates the institution of the Lord's Supper because it was also on this night that Jesus gave his disciples (and the church) the Sacrament of his body and blood. The **liturgical color** for the day is either scarlet or white. See also **Triduum.**

Mensa: The top surface of the **altar.** The term *mensa* is a Latin word meaning "table." This word reflects part of the altar's function, namely, that it is the table from which the Lord feeds us in his Holy Supper.

Minor Festivals: Lesser festivals which commemorate certain events in the life of our Lord (Circumcision, Presentation, Annunciation, Visitation), saints and martyrs, and certain events in the life of the church. See also **church year** and **major festivals.**

Missal: See **altar book.**

Missal stand: A stand of metal or wood on which the altar book sits during the service. It is removed from the altar when not in use.

Morning Prayer: See **Matins.**

Napkin: See **baptismal towel.**

Narthex: The entryway leading from the outside of the church building into the **nave.** The narthex is located at the liturgical **west** end of the building.

Nativity of Our Lord: After Easter the most important **major festival** of the **church year,** because it celebrates the coming of the Son of God into the flesh so that he could achieve the redemption of sinful man. Also known as Christmas, this festival is the central feast during the Time of Christmas. Its season extends from Christmas Eve until the Eve of the **Epiphany of Our Lord.** The color for the day and season is white.

Nave: The large, central area of the church building where the congregation gathers for the service. In traditional churches the nave contains two or more rows of pews from front to back. Many churches of more modern architectural style have chairs which can be arranged or moved depending on what kind of service is held. To the **east** of the nave is the **chancel** and to the **west** is the **narthex.**

North: See **east.**

Occasional Service: A service which celebrates a significant occasion in the life of congregational members or of the church. These services include **Marriage, Burial of the Dead,** dedication of a church, congregational anniversary, ordination, mission festivals, harvest festivals, and days of repentance and prayer. An occasional service may be held on any day except that of a **major festival.**

Octave: The day of a festival and the seven days which follow it, amounting to a total of eight days. Originally the festival was celebrated again on the eighth day, but that custom has fallen into disuse.

Office: The ordinary weekday prayer services of the church, ordinarily held in the morning and evening. Also called daily prayer. In the Lutheran tradition there are at least two offices: **Matins** and **Vespers.** See also **Compline** and **canonical hours.**

Office lights: Candles that are lighted for the conduct of the **offices.** Often these were candelabra with three, five, or seven branches which sat on the altar or on the floor near the altar in addition to the **eucharistic lights.** Today, preferred placement, with raised stands, is on the floor. See also **torch.**

Officiant: See **presiding minister.**

Ordinary: (1) A term used to refer to an unchanging sung or spoken part of the **Divine Service.** The ordinaries are the following: Kyrie, Gloria in Excelsis, Creed, Sanctus, and Agnus Dei. (2) A word which is used to describe the time of the **church year** in which the events in the life of Christ are not being celebrated, also referred to as "green" time. See also **propers.**

Orphrey: An ornamental band of a **parament** or **vestment** which coordinates with the **liturgical color** of the **church year.**

Pall: See **chalice pall** and **funeral pall.**

Palm Sunday: The Sunday before Easter and the first day of **Holy Week.** Palm Sunday commemorates the triumphal entry of Jesus into Jerusalem, which preceded his humiliation and death but also prefigured his glorious victory as the risen and ascended King. Also called Passion Sunday or Sunday of the Passion.

Paraments: Cloth hangings for the furnishings of the **chancel** which indicate the day or season of the **church year** by the **liturgical colors.** Ordinarily they are made of silk, satin, or some other fine material. Also see: **antependium, burse, chalice veil, frontal, frontlet, orphrey,** and **superfrontal.**

Paschal candle: A large candle used on Easter and during its season to indicate that Christ "the Light of the world" is risen from the dead. It is also used in a service for the **Burial of the Dead** and for services in which the Sacrament of **Holy Baptism** is administered, as a reminder that the life of the Christian only has meaning in view of the resurrection of Christ from the dead.

Passion Sunday: See **Palm Sunday.**

Paten: A round plate to hold the sacramental **hosts** of the service of **Holy Communion.** Normally it is the sacramental vessel on which the communion breads are consecrated and from which they are distributed. The paten should be of a size which allows it to sit on top of the **chalice** when the chalice is vested.

Pectoral cross: A **cross** which is attached to a chain and suspended over the neck. Historically the pectoral cross was worn by a bishop to indicate his office.

Pentecost: A **major festival** of the **church year** which celebrates Christ's sending of the Holy Spirit to his apostles so that they could carry on his work and establish his church. Pentecost falls on the fiftieth day after Easter. The **liturgical color** is red.

Pietism: A religious movement of the 17th and 18th centuries in Germany. Pietism stressed emotion over the objective means of grace to the point of disregarding the sacraments. It led to the infrequent celebration of the Lord's Supper, contrary to the historic Lutheran practice of celebrating the Lord's Supper every Sunday, or Lord's Day.

Piscina: A basin in the sacristy with a drain pipe leading into the ground. It is used for disposing of consecrated wine that was not consumed in the Lord's Supper and of water that was used for Holy Baptism.

Post-Communion veil: A white linen cloth that is sometimes used instead of the **chalice veil** to drape over the chalice and paten after the celebration of Holy Communion.

Predella: A raised platform, usually one or two steps above the floor of the **chancel,** on which the **altar** sits. It is sometimes also called a footpace.

Presiding minister: The chief minister or officiant, particularly in the **Divine Service** but also in other services as well. The portions of the **liturgy** which must be done by the presiding minister are the **Absolution** at the beginning of the service, the **Collect** of the Day, the reading of the Holy Gospel, the consecration of the elements in **Holy Communion,** and the Benediction at the end of the service. The presiding minister must be an ordained clergyman. He ordinarily wears a **stole** as a mark of his office. Sometimes also called the celebrant. Recent understanding, however, of the corporate nature of both the church and its worship considers the congregation as the celebrant, and the ordained pastor as the presider, or presiding minister, not as one who celebrates on behalf of or apart from the faithful. Thus, the term *celebrant* does not appear in *Lutheran Worship* (1982) nor in its companion volumes. See also **assisting minister.**

Prie dieu: A piece of **chancel** furniture that looks like an individual kneeler with a shelf to hold service books. Also called a kneeling desk. The prie dieu is often positioned in front of the **sedile.** It may also be placed at the head of the **nave** for individuals to kneel at in the service of Corporate Confession and Absolution.

Priest's host: See **celebrant's host.**

Procession: A **ceremony** in which a person or group of persons move from one point to another. Often it is accompanied by music and singing. There are several kinds of processions. One procession is the entrance rite, when the ministers and **servers** march from the **narthex** to the **chancel.** In the **Gospel procession** the **presiding minister** and servers carry the **lectionary** or **Gospel book** into the middle of the **nave** for the reading of the Holy Gospel. In a funeral procession the ministers and people accompany the coffin to the place of interment.

Processional cross: A **cross** or **crucifix** (preferable) mounted on a standard and carried at the head of a **procession.**

Processional torch: A large candle mounted on a standard and carried in a **procession.** See also **torch.**

Propers: The parts of the **liturgy** which change from week to week and festival day to festival day. The propers are the Introit, **Collect** of the Day, Psalm of the Day, Gradual, readings, and Hymn of the Day. See also **ordinary.**

Protector linen: A linen that is placed over the **mensa** of the **altar** before the **fair linen** in order to protect the fair linen. See **cerecloth.**

Pulpit: A principal piece of liturgical furniture with the **altar** and **font.** The pulpit is the place of the Word. Ordinarily the sermon is preached from the pulpit, but the readings may be read from there as well.

Pulpit gown: A black gown that is sometimes worn by the minister. Also called a Geneva gown. Although **vestments** are an **adiaphoron,** the pulpit gown is an inappropriate form of dress, since it is academic and not ecclesiastical in character.

Purificator: One of the sacramental linens. It serves to wipe the rim of the **chalice** after use. In setting up the sacramental vessels, the purificator is placed over the chalice and under the **paten** when the chalice is being vested. Usually several additional purificators are put in the **burse** or laid on the **corporal** next to the vested chalice.

Pyx: A small round or rectangular container with a cover that is used to hold **hosts.** See also **ciborium.**

Reredos: A piece of wood or stone that is built onto the wall behind the **altar** as an ornamental backdrop for the altar. Instead of a reredos the altar may have a **dossal.**

Resurrection of Our Lord: The chief festival of the **church year.** On this day the church celebrates the rising of her Lord from the dead. This festival is also called Easter. The date of Easter changes from year to year and is arrived at with the following formula: the first Sunday after the first full moon after the spring equinox. The **liturgical color** for the day is white, but gold is an appropriate alternative. See also **Vigil of Easter.**

Retable: See **gradine.**

Rite: Technically rite is the combination of **ceremony** (action) and **liturgy** (text). For example, the rite of **Holy Baptism,** or the rite of **confirmation.** Often the term is used as a synonym of ceremony. Rite can also be used as a synonym of liturgy. The "Western rite" is the form of the **Divine Service** that is common to the churches descended from the Roman church.

Rubric: A rule or guide for conducting the **liturgy.** The term comes from *ruber,* the Latin word for "red." In early service books instructions on how to conduct the liturgy were written in red ink.

Sacrament: A sacred **rite** in which God offers his grace and bestows the forgiveness of sins. One definition of the term (a sacred act, instituted by God, and attached to a visible **element**) limits the number of sacraments to two: **Holy Baptism** and **Holy Communion.** A broader definition, implied in the **Lutheran Confessions** (Apology, Article XIII; Large Catechism, Part IV) includes Holy **Absolution** as a sacrament. Sometimes the phrase "the Sacrament" is used as a synonym for Holy Communion.

Sacristy: A room near the **chancel** where **paraments, vestments,** linens, the sacramental vessels, and other supplies are kept and in which the altar guild does some of its work. See also **vestry.**

Sanctuary: The part of the **chancel** where the **altar** is located. Sometimes it is set off from the **choir** by an **altar rail.** In popular usage the term is used to refer to the entire area in which services are held, namely, the chancel and the **nave** together.

Sanctuary light: A candle that burns continuously in the **chancel.** Originally its purpose was to indicate the presence of the reserved **Sacrament.** Today it is thought to symbolize the presence of God. Also called an "eternal light."

Sedile: A seat in the **chancel** on which a minister or server sits. The plural is "sedilia."

Server: In a general sense, any of those persons who assist the **presiding minister** in the service. Usually the term is limited to **acolyte, crucifer, thurifer,** and **torchbearer** and is not applied to the **assisting minister** or **lector.**

South: See **east.**

Stole: A **vestment** worn by an ordained clergyman to signify his office. The stole is a long band of material that hangs over the neck and down the front. It is the same color as the **paraments.**

Sunday of the Passion: See **Palm Sunday.**

Superfrontal: A **parament** which covers the front of the **altar.** It is shorter than the **frontal,** hanging down only 8–12 inches from the **mensa.** See also **frontlet.**

Surplice: A white **vestment** worn over the **cassock.** The surplice has long, wide sleeves and extends to below the knees. See also **cotta.**

Tenebrae: A traditional service held on **Good Friday** in which candles are individually extinguished in the course of a series of readings.

Thurible: A vessel with a perforated cover for burning **incense.** A piece of charcoal is ignited and placed in the thurible and over it grains of incense are sprinkled. The thurible is then swung to disperse the smoke.

Thurifer: The **server** who carries the **thurible.**

Torch: A candle mounted on a standard. It is usually carried in **procession.** Two torches may flank the **altar,** where they would serve as **eucharistic lights** instead of candles sitting on the **altar.** A torch may be placed next to the **lectern** or reading desk (or two may flank it) for one of the **offices.** In this instance it would serve as an **office light.**

Torchbearer: The **server** who carries a **torch.**

Transept: In a church whose floor plan is the shape of a cross, the horizontal "arms" are called transepts. Sometimes a church is built with only one transept.

Transfiguration of Our Lord: A **major festival** of the **church year** occurring as the last Sunday after the **Epiphany.** The festival commemorates the event in our Lord's life when he took Peter, James, and John up onto the mountain and revealed his divine glory to them as a preview of the glory of the resurrected Christ. The color for this festival is white.

Triduum: A term used to refer to three most sacred days—**Maundy Thursday, Good Friday,** and **Holy Saturday.** This three-day period is viewed as a single liturgical event, which culminates in the **Vigil** or **Easter.**

Vase: A vessel used to hold flowers. It may be placed on the **gradine** of the altar or on a flower stand that sits on the floor.

Veil: See **chalice veil, Post-Communion veil,** and **Lenten veil.**

Vespers: The evening weekday **office** of daily prayer. This office consists of psalmody, a reading from Scripture, a hymn, sermon, canticle, and prayers. Historically the sermon was not part of the daily prayer office, but with Luther's emphasis on the proclamation of the

Word it has received a place in the Lutheran tradition of the office. Sometimes Vespers is also called "Evening Prayer," although the two services can be distinct in theme and structure. See also **canonical hours.**

Vestments: Garments worn by those performing liturgical duties in the **Divine Service** and other services. The liturgical purpose of vestments is to mark the person who is performing specific liturgical functions, such as the **presiding minister, assisting minister,** and **servers.** See also: **alb, cassock, chasuble, cincture, cope, cotta, orphrey, stole,** and **surplice.**

Vestry: The place where the minister and his assistants put on their **vestments.** Sometimes the vestry is a separate room; sometimes the **sacristy** serves as the vestry.

Vigil of Easter: A service held on the Eve of Easter or early Easter morning before sunrise to celebrate the **Resurrection of Our Lord.** The Vigil consists of four parts: the Service of Light, the Service of Readings, the Service of Holy Baptism, and the Service of Holy Communion. The Vigil begins in quiet darkness and gradually increases in light and celebratory praise, although it should be less festive than the main service on Easter Day. See also **Triduum.**

Wafer: See **host.**

Water: See **elements.**

West: See **east.**

Wine: See **elements.**

F
Bibliography

General Works

Lamburn, E. C. R. *Ritual Notes: A Comprehensive Guide to the Rites and Ceremonies of the Book of Common Prayer of the English Church*. London: W. Knott and Son Limited, 1964.

Precht, Fred L., ed. *Lutheran Worship: History and Practice*. St. Louis: Concordia Publishing House, 1993.

Talley, Thomas J. *The Origins of the Liturgical Year*. Collegeville, MN: The Liturgical Press, 1991.

Wegman, Herman. *Christian Worship in East and West: A Study Guide to Liturgical History*. Translated by Gordon W. Lathrop. Collegeville, MN: The Liturgical Press, 1990.

Reference Works

Davies, John Gordon. *The New Westminster Dictionary of Liturgy and Worship*. Philadelphia: Westminster Press, 1986.

Lutheran Worship Agenda. The Commission on Worship of The Lutheran Church—Missouri Synod. St. Louis: Concordia Publishing House, 1984.

Lutheran Worship Altar Book. The Commission on Worship of The Lutheran Church—Missouri Synod. St. Louis: Concordia Publishing House, 1982.

Altar Guild Manuals

Gebauer, Victor. *Manual for Altar Guilds*. Minneapolis: Augsburg Publishing House, 1986.

Lang, Paul H. D. *What an Altar Guild Should Know*. St. Louis: Concordia Publishing House, 1964.

Stauffer, S. Anita. *Altar Guild Handbook*. Philadelphia: Fortress Press, 1985.

Church Art and Architecture

Bishops' Committee on the Liturgy. *Environment and Art in Catholic Worship*. Washington, DC: National Conference of Catholic Bishops, 1978.

Caemmerer, Richard R., Jr. *Visual Art in the Life of the Church*. Minneapolis: Augsburg Publishing House, 1983.

Huffman, Walter C. and Stauffer, S. Anita. *Where We Worship*. Prepared under the auspices of the Association of Evangelical Lutheran Churches; Division for Life and Mission in the Congregation, The American Lutheran Church; Division for Parish Life, Evangelical Lutheran Church in Canada; Division for Parish Services, Lutheran Church in America; and Commission on Worship, The Lutheran Church—Missouri Synod. Philadelphia: Board of Publications, Lutheran Church in America, 1987.

Walton, Janet R. *Art and Worship: A Vital Connection*. Wilmington, DE: Michael Glazier, 1988.

Christian Symbols

Bradner, John. *Symbols of Church Seasons and Days*. Wilton, CN: Morehouse-Barlow, 1977.

Sill, Gertrude Grace. *A Handbook of Symbols in Christian Art*. New York: Macmillan Publishing Company, 1975.

Banners and Embroidery

Bargmann, Dale A. *Raise a Banner to the Lord*. St. Louis: Concordia Publishing House, 1993.

Dean, Beryl. *Church Embroidery*. Wilton, CN: Morehouse-Barlow, 1984.

DeBord, Jane and Isbell, Linda. *Banner Designs for Celebrating Christians*. St. Louis: Concordia Publishing House, 1984.

Harms, Carol Jean. *Banners for Worship*. St. Louis: Concordia Publishing House, 1988. (Patterns available, CPH order number: 12-3114)

_____, *Quick & Easy Banner Designs*. St. Louis: Concordia Publishing House, 1996.

G

Index

Altar Guild Members

Name_____

Address _____

Phone (home)_____

(work) _____

Name_____

Address _____

Phone (home)_____

(work) _____

Name_____

Address _____

Phone (home)_____

(work) _____

Name_____

Address _____

Phone (home)_____

(work) _____

Name_____

Address _____

Phone (home)_____

(work) _____

Name_____

Address _____

Phone (home)_____

(work) _____

Name_____

Address _____

Phone (home)_____

(work) _____

Name_____

Address _____

Phone (home)_____

(work) _____

Name_____

Address _____

Phone (home)_____

(work) _____

Name_____

Address _____

Phone (home)_____

(work) _____

Name_____

Address _____

Phone (home)_____

(work) _____

Name_____

Address _____

Phone (home)_____

(work) _____

Name_____

Address _____

Phone (home)_____

(work) _____

Name_____

Address _____

Phone (home)_____

(work) _____

Name_____

Address _____

Phone (home)_____

    (work) _____

Name_____

Address _____

Phone (home)_____

    (work) _____

Name_____

Address _____

Phone (home)_____

    (work) _____

Name_____

Address _____

Phone (home)_____

    (work) _____

Name_____

Address _____

Phone (home)_____

    (work) _____

Name_____

Address _____

Phone (home)_____

    (work) _____

Name_____

Address _____

Phone (home)_____

    (work) _____

Name_____

Address _____

Phone (home)_____

    (work) _____

Name_____

Address _____

Phone (home)_____

    (work) _____

Name_____

Address _____

Phone (home)_____

    (work) _____

Name_____

Address _____

Phone (home)_____

    (work) _____

Name_____

Address _____

Phone (home)_____

    (work) _____

Name_____

Address _____

Phone (home)_____

    (work) _____

Name_____

Address _____

Phone (home)_____

    (work) _____

Name_____

Address _____

Phone (home)_____

     (work) _____

Name_____

Address _____

Phone (home)_____

     (work) _____

Name_____

Address _____

Phone (home)_____

     (work) _____

Name_____

Address _____

Phone (home)_____

     (work) _____

Name_____

Address _____

Phone (home)_____

     (work) _____

Name_____

Address _____

Phone (home)_____

     (work) _____

Name_____

Address _____

Phone (home)_____

     (work) _____

Name_____

Address _____

Phone (home)_____

     (work) _____

Name_____

Address _____

Phone (home)_____

     (work) _____

Name_____

Address _____

Phone (home)_____

     (work) _____

Name_____

Address _____

Phone (home)_____

     (work) _____

Name_____

Address _____

Phone (home)_____

     (work) _____

SUNDAY	MONDAY	TUESDAY	WEDNESDAY	THURSDAY	FRIDAY	SATURDAY

Notes

Notes

Notes